The 7 Fatal Mistakes
Divorced & Separated
Parents Make:

Strategies for Raising Healthy
Children of Divorce and Conflict

Shannon R. Rios, MS LMFT

LifeThreads Books
Evergreen, Colorado

Editing, cover and interior design by
Black Cat Creative Services, Cleveland, OH
www.blackcateditor.com

Manufactured in the United States of America

10   9   8   7   6   5   4   3   2   1

Library of Congress Cataloging-in-Publication Data

Rios, Shannon R.
   The 7 fatal mistakes divorced and separated parents make: strategies for raising healthy children of divorce and conflict / by Shannon R. Rios
   256p. cm.

   Includes bibliographic index and reference notes
   1. Divorce.   2. Parenting.   3. Child development.

ISBN: 978-0-615-31495-2

Library of Congress Control Number: 2009908509

Testimonials

"This book is outstanding! It contains not only extremely valuable information every parent facing divorce needs to know, but it also is full of practical tools for minimizing the impact of divorce on children. I highly recommend it."

—Judge Stephen A. Groome, District Judge,
11th Judicial District, State of Colorado

"This wonderful book should be required reading and writing for every divorced or never-married parent. It also should be on the bookshelf of every mediator, counselor or attorney helping separated parents raise happier kids."

—Dr. Shirley Thomas, author of *Two Happy Homes: A Working Guide for Parents & Stepparents After Divorce and Remarriage*

"Don't let the word *Fatal* in the title scare you. When you look inside, you will find Shannon Rios's book to be one of the best parenting-after-divorce books ever written. She has understanding, compassion, and an uncanny understanding of what children—and parents—need. I have seen many divorce books during the past 25 years, and while they are all helpful in varying degrees, if every parent read Shannon's book, most of the problems suffered by children as an outcome of their parents' divorce would be substantially eased. This book should be required reading in all divorce classes."

—David L. Levy, Esq., President, Board of Trustees,
Children's Rights Council

"This book is a must-read for parents contemplating divorce, those already in the divorce process, and those who have a parenting plan in place. It gives parents important insight into the issues and real needs of children. Shannon has very important knowledge and wisdom to share with parents. I will recommend this book to all my clients who are dealing with parenting plan issues."

—Albert V. Evans, Family Law attorney since 1970

"Every so often someone comes along with the rare ability to see things differently and in doing so, changes our lives forever. Suddenly, issues that seemed so difficult to understand and actions that seemed too painful to take, begin to open up to an entirely new understanding that shifts our consciousness and heals our soul! It is this clarity of vision that Shannon Rios brings to her latest work. You owe it to yourself to read this powerful new book but more importantly, you owe it to your children."

—Jeffrey Alan Hall, author, speaker, teacher,
www.jeffreyalenhall.com, A Course in Miracles

"Shannon Rios's personal experience, research, and professional expertise offer compassion and respect to divorced and separated parents. If parents read *The Fatal 7 Mistakes* and apply all the practical tips this book offers, they will get along better with their parenting partners, heal from their divorce faster and help their children come through the divorce with their self-esteem intact. This book will help ensure families achieve emotional health despite these life-changing events."

—Jody Johnston Pawel, author of the award-winning book, *The Parent's Toolshop: The Universal Blueprint for Building a Healthy Family*

"Shannon comes from personal experience and from the heart in her deep desire to help children of divorcing parents. Parents— read this book! You CAN move through the divorce process without injuring your children!"

—Margaret Paul, Ph.D., author/coauthor of *Healing Your Aloneness, Inner Bonding, Do I Have To Give Up Me To Be Loved By You?*, and *Do I Have To Give Up Me To Be Loved By God?*

"For the divorced or separated parent who wants to raise emotionally safe and secure children: this book is a very important resource. This book was easy to read, yet practically applicable, capable of bringing out the subtle actions and words that parents, hurting from their own divorce experience, may not realize are inadvertently hurting their children."

—David Meggitt, Manager, Colorado Children's Program
Betty Ford Institute

"This book is a key practical tool for parents when life is in crisis. It will help to ensure that our unresolved issues start healing and do not dim the possibility of a joyful and creative life for our children. I truly thank you for gifting this book to the world."

—Candice Bataille Popiel, co-parent of a 7- and 8-year old and co-author of *Discovery of Glow*

"Parents of separation, divorce and conflict will find this book an invaluable and treasured guide—it's filled with heart-felt, sage, and practical advice. Shannon Rios shows parents how to ask themselves and their children questions that optimize healing and growth, even during times of conflict and difficulty. Children whose parents read this book will be lucky indeed!"

—Marilee Adams, PhD, author of *Change Your Questions, Change Your Life: 10 Powerful Tools for Life and Work*

"As a mother of a 7-year old and going through a divorce, my main concern is the well-being of my child. This book is a godsend! It has helped me be the best mom for my son, while going through this difficult process."

—Katy, mother of a 7-year old

"Divorced and divorcing parents and their children, regardless of age, will see themselves in this book. They will also recognize the author knows how easy it is to be ensnared in the traps she describes and how difficult it is to avoid them. Shannon provides many prompts for improving self awareness and exercises to aid management of tendencies harmful to children. Those able to follow at least some of her suggestions should be richly rewarded by improvement in the health and happiness of their children as well themselves."

—Bonnie W. Camp, MD, PhD, Professor Emeritus, Pediatrics and Psychiatry, University of Colorado School of Medicine

Dedication

To every child of
divorce and conflict in this world,
May your pain be healed.

To my parents,
thank you for this journey
so that I may assist others.

To my sisters,
Jessica and Karissa,
I love you both so very much.

And my nephew, Liam,
thank you for your joy.

Acknowledgements

I would like to thank my friends and family who assisted me in making this book possible. Thank you, Karla, for your countless edits and "2-cents-worth" of million-dollar ideas. Thanks to my sister, Karissa who always assisted with her thoughts and opinions. Thank you to Phillip, who was a technical wizard and a great support. Thank you to Randy, my editor and constant support in this project, your patience and collaboration is a gift. Thank you to all my friends who gave me feedback on this book, you know who you are.

Finally, thank you to my parents. I thank you for allowing me to share our family's story so that we may assist others. I thank you for your support and blessings in writing this book.

Contents

Introduction

Growing up a child of conflict and divorce, I would never in a million years have imagined myself working with families of divorce. As I began to put this book together, I felt some mixed emotions: sadness as I recalled the pain and conflict I experienced as a child, yet excitement for the hope and help I planned to share through the book. As I was writing my business plan for the coming year, I asked myself, "Is this type of work truly my passion? I am 36-years old, single and have never been married. So why in the world would I want to focus my energy on writing this book?" The truth is that I want to assist you in shielding your children from pain, hurt and heartache. I know I cannot save the world, but I do know I am here for a purpose, which is to assist in creating healthier families so we can have healthier and happier children. So obviously I made the decision to write this book and I am clear in my heart that I was meant to write it. It has been a complete honor to share my knowledge and to assist families.

When I teach my divorce-education class and see the light go on for parents when they realize how their behavior is impacting their children, my heart is happy. If I help just one child have less anxiety, have better social relationships, be a better partner and parent or just enjoy their childhood more, I can be satisfied that I have done my work. My mind used to want to go to the big picture of impacting, now I just focus on the present, one child at a time. I have a huge heart for children and I know I have been given this vision around children, families and divorce. I make a difference in children's lives, one child at a time.

I am writing this book for you, parents who are divorced, going through a divorce, or considering a divorce. You may also be a co-parent who has never been married to your child's other parent, you too will find this book helpful. It is time for me to share the knowledge that I have gained from my own parents' divorce and conflict, from the parents I have trained, from the children I have counseled, and from the divorces of friends and family. My wish for you and your family is healing, health and love. My deepest hope is that this book will bring you and your family one step closer to these goals. If what I am sharing assists you in any way to positively impact your family, I know I have done my work here and I am deeply satisfied.

I want to take this time to honor you for picking up this book. In picking up and reading this book, you also want to positively contribute during your time here. You are interested in creating a better society through your own actions. I know this time can feel so painful *and* that you are making a step to move beyond your pain for the greater good of your children. You want what is best for your children and you are willing to at least explore taking positive action. I thank you for that because you don't have to read this book. You are special. I promise you, if you take action on even some of the suggestions in this book, you will raise children who will be emotionally and physically healthier than they otherwise would have been. They will have an easier life due to your decision to take action in your own life. This is truly the greatest gift you can give to your children. Your children will thank you. Truly, your children do not want material gifts, they want healthy parents and families who love them. I would return every gift my parents ever gave me in return for less conflict and more love in our family.

This book is written from in-depth knowledge and experience with the subject matter. It is also written from my heart. I have no other motive in writing about this topic except the best interests of my readers. May you receive everything you are meant to receive from this book to allow you and your family to heal and move forward in the best way possible for your children. From my heart to yours, I thank you for who you are and for the parent you are for your children. You know they deserve the best parent possible through this event (divorce) that they did not choose. I thank you for being that parent.

My Story

At age 29, after a six-year corporate career as an human resource manager, my job was eliminated. In a meeting with a career counselor, I answered a question on her form. The question was, "What do you know the most about? What would you want to talk on national television for one hour about?" My answer was, "children and divorce." At that moment, something shifted and my life changed. I became 100% clear about what I was truly in this world to do.

My parents first went through divorce proceedings when I was 11. I remember a police car coming to our home to serve divorce papers. They reconciled and had my youngest sister who is 13-years younger than me. I remember thinking at age 13, "What are they doing? Why are they bringing another person into this mess of conflict and anger?" I even told my mom that if she had another child, I would leave.

I have two younger sisters, one 11-years younger and one 13-years younger than me. I want to say that they are the biggest blessings in my life and I am so happy they are with me today. When my sisters were nine- and 11-years old and I was 21, my parents officially divorced. My sisters called me on the phone to let me know that our dad had moved out for good. I knew first-hand the fear and pain they were feeling. I watched as my sisters endured the turmoil of my parents' divorce. My parents' marriage and divorce was and still is riddled with conflict and anger. I really have no happy memories of my family being together. During that time of my family's transition, I tried to assist my sisters in the best way I could, but I was also dealing with all of my own feelings.

At that same time, I was dating a wonderful guy. The following year, his family endured an unbelievable divorce full of lies, an affair, a suicide attempt, and a lot of pain. His younger sister was 16 and I saw the pain and hurt she endured from her parents' selfishness when they put her in the middle of their relationship issues. My then boyfriend's younger sister was the most amazing kid and it felt so unfair to me. It was like she was being punished for something she had no role in whatsoever. It hurt me to see her parents hurt her that way.

The next divorce I experienced came when I was 24. My cousin, who is my age, divorced her husband. She and I had been good friends as kids. She had two girls, then aged 5 and 3, and a baby on the way. Her divorce included each parent being arrested, violence, and a terrible custody battle. My cousin lost custody of her children. I remember being so concerned for those two girls; I knew first hand that they were experiencing extreme pain and fear. I became an emotional support for the girls throughout their growing years. The girls are now 16 and 14 and have reunited with mom.

Divorce is intriguing to me due to the various situations I have witnessed and directly experienced. From those experiences though, I believe if a divorce must happen, that there is a better way to do it than how I (and some people) have experienced it. Children should always be put first. I believe that if parents can heal their own relationship wounds, they can then create a positive parenting relationship with their co-parent.

This book certainly does not have all the answers. It will give you a vision of what you can do so that you can be the best parent possible for your children to assist them during this difficult time that was not of their choosing. My ultimate goal is your success as a parent. And your success directly correlates to your child's success. As I said, my goal here is to help one child at a time. I ask you to assist me in achieving this vision.

At the point that I realized I wanted to work with children and families of divorce, I knew it would be a journey. I saw I would need over two years of schooling and probably two more to get my marriage and family therapy license. It seemed so far away then. I have now been working in the profession for six years. I am impacting children and I know I have made the right choice. I am now a licensed marriage and family therapist practicing with families of divorce and conflict. I am also a life coach and management leadership coach. I have not yet had my own family. Honestly, I had so much to work through on my own and to let go of before I was ready to be a good partner and mother. Having my own family is one of my dreams in life. I believe that dream has been put on hold for now so I could focus my energy to assist you and your children. It is my honor and privilege to have this opportunity in this lifetime. What I ask in return is that you be open to the suggestions in this book and that you focus on taking responsibility for your own actions. I ask you to read this book with an open heart and mind and to put your children first. I thank you for reading this book. I thank you for being a good parent. I thank you for putting your child first.

I want to include here that I believe that if you have created a family with someone, you should do all that is possible to make your family work—seek family counseling to talk with an objective professional to work through the issues stressing your relationship and/or marriage. The work to heal your relationship will take time and commitment. I believe this process is preferable to divorce/separation even if you were never married but are co-parenting. But, in many cases, reconciliation is not possible. And it is for children of those families that I have written this book. They will be impacted forever by this event. Your actions will determine just how they are impacted.

I also wrote this book for parents who were never married and are now co-parenting (this population is growing). This book will assist you in understanding some of the events and situations you will encounter. As we all know, every relationship has it's own story. My only goal is to positively impact the story of your co-parenting relationship.

Throughout the book, I draw on my private practice cases and personal experiences with divorce. The cases I discuss are about real families, real people. I have significantly altered personal details about individuals to ensure that their identities and right to confidentiality are protected.

Finally, closing each chapter, are open pages for you to make any notes or to write your own reflections on what you are reading. Journaling is an excellent method of expressing yourself so you can become clearer on what is important in your life. I have also included a couple of journaling questions at the end of each chapter if you need assistance getting started. You may also want to purchase a notebook to ensure you have all the space that you need to fully express yourself and to do the exercises in the book.

Exercises are also included in this book and a workbook will be published in the future. It is crucial to actually do these exercises as they will help you process where you have been and where you want to go with your life. There are also exercises to write down your goals and these are crucial because once you write down your goals you are much more likely to achieve them. I have included all of these aspects to assist you in being successful as you read this book and make this journey. Your success is my success. My goal is to give you every opportunity through my words and the exercises in this book to allow you to be a successful co-parent for your child.

Questions For Reflection:

Why is it important for me to read this book and complete the exercises?

_____

_____

_____

_____

_____

We all have some kind of story that explains where we are today. What are the biggest aspects of my story so far in my life?

_____

_____

_____

_____

_____

What do I want my future story to be?

_____

_____

_____

_____

_____

_____

_____

_____

_____

~~|~~

Creating The Future First

This book's title, *The 7 Fatal Mistakes Divorced and Separated Parents Make,* does not reflect an optimistic outlook. Honestly, deep in my heart I am an optimist, and I want to start this book on that note. The truth is, if you really take into account what this book says, there is so much hope for you and your children. If you choose to, you will be able to live into the reality of the subtitle, "Strategies for Raising Healthy Children of Divorce and Conflict." To this end, I begin this book with hope. When we have hope, all things are possible. I recently heard that those who are the most depressed and feel like life is futile have lost hope. Divorce is incredibly challenging because we feel we are losing control and there are so many unknowns. So many thoughts go through our minds, "Will our children love us? Will we make it financially? Will we ever find another partner?" Life can seem futile and like there is no hope. I want to reassure you that you are in control of two very key aspects of your and your child's future. The two areas you do have major influence and control over are:

1. Your child's future—their relationships, self-esteem and happiness
2. Your relationship with your child

The choices you make right now and into the next days, months and years will lay the foundation for the two outcomes above. Even if you are well along into your divorce, you can still impact the above two items. I guarantee you that even 15 years after their divorce, my parents sometimes still impact our relationship negatively or positively by their behavior; positive changes in their behavior can still positively impact our relationship. So, given the critical impact you have on your children, I ask you to commit 8–10 hours of work now in the best interests of you and your child. I believe it will take you 8–10 hours to thoroughly read this book and complete the exercises. This is just one day of your time. Throughout this book, I ask you to take time to complete some exercises and answer questions. I also have given you space at the end of each chapter to reflect on what you have read.

As a life coach, I ask you to commit to this time right now. I ask you to make a commitment to your and your child's lives. You may never know the exact effect that these changes in your behavior will have. However, I can guarantee that by taking the time to complete the exercises and answer the questions thoughtfully and honestly, you will in some measure impact the following:

+ Your child's ability to have more successful relationships with their peers.
+ Your child's ability to live easier and in more peace.
+ Your child's ability to feel more safe and secure.
+ Your child's ability to secure more easily a wonderful partner for themselves if they choose this.
+ Your ability to have a more loving relationship with your child.

Is it worth it? I ask you now to make a choice. Are the successful outcomes of the five areas mentioned above important enough for me to invest 8–10 hours to complete the activities in this book? If your answer is yes, and I am going to assume it is since you picked up this book, please read this statement aloud:

The success of my child and my relationship with my child is so important that I am willing to invest 8–10 hours to read and complete the activities in this book. I know that I will positively impact my child's life by completing these exercises. I also know at times this may be challenging, but as a parent, this is a challenge I can fully embrace. I am so thankful my child is in my life. I am so thankful for this opportunity to be the best parent possible for my child during this difficult time in our lives.

With this commitment in mind, I ask you now to answer in writing the following two questions (please be sure to write your responses in the space below):

1. What do you want for your child's future?

_____

_____

_____

2. What do you want for your future relationship with your child?

_____

_____

_____

Read right now what you have just written. You hold the power to directly impact these two areas. During this time of divorce in your family, I ask you to choose now to do your very best at this job. I ask you to take this job more seriously than any other job you've held in your life. Read this book and implement the ideas in it for yourself, for your children and for their children. Decide now to take action to be the best parent possible, it is the most important job you will ever do.

At this time, I am going to ask you to complete a vision for your family. It is time now to begin to see you and your child as your family. The sooner you see you and your child/ren as a family, the faster they will make that transition. If you have decided to divorce or separate, it is now time to let go of your old attachments to that other person. You are a family with your child. You simply just don't have the other parent in your family. Your child, on the other hand, now has two families. If you decide to, you can choose to maintain a family atmosphere with the other parent even though you are divorced. And we will discuss how you can do that later in the book. This can occur if you are a cooperative parent with your child's other parent. No matter what your relationship with your child's other parent, I ask you to separately create your own family vision for you and your child/ren. I also suggest that you involve your children in creating the vision for your family.

Vision For My Family

Exercise 2 What is it that you want to create in your new family? What is the vision that you have for your new family (write this in the space below)?

_____

_____

_____

_____

_____

Example: *My family vision is that we will create a space of love, laughter, support and communication together. We will always respect each other and spend quality time together. If we have frustrations, we will communicate about those and work toward a positive outcome for everyone. We will tell each other that we love each other and will hug each other each day.*

Now that you have looked into the future and imagined the future you want with your child, your child's future and your vision for your family, let's move into the steps you can take to ensure you create this in your life. If you truly want the above vision to manifest for you, the secrets lie in this book.

Single Parent vs. Co-Parent

As you read this book, you may notice terms that I use repeatedly, these are *co-parent* or *your child's other parent*. It is better for your child if you refer to this important person in his or her life in a more positive manner than *your ex* or *your former spouse*. Truly, co-parent is their new role relative to you now, they are your child's *other parent*. I also must mention here that unless you have no idea where your child's other parent is or you are parenting a child completely solo, you are not a single parent. It concerns me when I hear co-parents refer to themselves as single parents when they really are not. If your child has another parent in the picture in any way, your child is not a one-parent child. This is what you are saying when you say single parent. That term is reserved for people who have no other parent helping them in anyway. If you are referring to yourself this way, please rethink it; hearing this negatively impacts your child's feelings of safety and security. They are not a child of a single parent. They know they have two parents. It is important that you also recognize and acknowledge your child's other parent's role as your co-parent.

Seven Reasons To Read This Book

I believe there are seven key reasons why it is crucial for you to read this book and complete the exercises.

1. Your actions during this time directly impact your child's emotional and physical health. Judith Wallerstein found in her long-term research that: *"The quality of the child's relationship with each parent and the relationship between parents are key factors in the child's emotional and social adjustment after divorce."*[1]

2. Unless your child proceeds you in death, you will be connected to your co-parent for your entire life. Make this as easy as possible for everyone involved. It is crucial that you learn to effectively co-parent.

3. Children of divorce have significantly more adjustment and achievement problems compared to those from non-divorced families. Children from divorced homes have more illnesses, medical problems, physicians visits and were also three times more likely to receive psychological treatment. Research also shows that 25% of children from divorced families have serious social, emotional and psychological problems, compared to 10% of children of non-divorced families.[2]

4. If you heal your own pain over the loss of your relationship, you will be able to be the best parent possible for your child.

5. Your child is counting on you to provide the best foundation and support possible for them to grow into a

successful adult. This is truly the most important job you will ever have.

6. One study reported that when parents related to each other in a healthy manner after divorce and conflict was low, their children in the long run, felt that they were better off or were not affected by their parents' divorce. This conclusion was based on a study of 173 adults who experienced divorce as children.[3]
7. You love your child and want to ensure their future success. You deserve the best life possible and so does your child.

In her book, *The Divorced Parent,* Stephanie Marston explains that to promote the healthy adjustment and development of your child, you must take the following actions:[4]

1. Protect your child from parents' disputes.
2. Allow your children to be free to love both parents.
3. Both parents must shift their role from intimate partners to parenting partners.
4. Allow your child to have access to both parents without being placed in loyalty conflicts.
5. Recover from the trauma of your unsuccessful relationship and rebuild.

If the above actions are not taken, the following results may occur:

1. Children are not well adjusted.
2. Children will do poorly in school.
3. Children are aggressive with peers, misbehave and develop psychological problems that will follow them into adulthood.
4. Your child will exhibit fear of abandonment or rejection.
5. Your child may be often unable to form and sustain significant adult relationships.

> **"You are the key to supporting and promoting your child's adjustment during and following the divorce."**
> —Nicolas Long, PhD & Rex Forehand, PhD

I know you want to learn how to take the top five actions so that the bottom five results don't happen to your children, so let's get started. I am clear that some things in this book will ring true immediately and others won't. At times the light bulb will go on and you will see something you never saw before. Awareness of old habits and patterns is the first step to creating new and healthy patterns for yourselves and your children. I wish you all the success in the world. May you and your children live in peace.

Questions For Reflection:

What can I do to positively impact my child?

_____

_____

_____

_____

What steps can I take to begin creating my family vision for my family?

_____

_____

_____

_____

Why is it important for me to take the time and read this book?

_____

_____

_____

_____

_____

_____

_____

_____

_____

_____

_____

_____

_____

~~2~~

Fatal Mistake #1: The Parent Basher— Saying Negative Things About Your Child's Other Parent Or Guardian

The Parent Basher Quiz:

You are a parent basher if you do any of the following:
- ❑ I sometimes say negative things to my child about their other parent.
- ❑ I sometimes get frustrated, verbally or non-verbally, in front of my child when my child's other parent does or says something that I do not like.
- ❑ I sometimes say negative things in front of my child about their other parent's new partner.
- ❑ I talk negatively to my friends and relatives on the phone about my child's other parent when my child is present (even if my child is in the other room as children have an ability to pick up on this).
- ❑ I quiz my child for anything negative that may have happened while they were in their other parent's care.
- ❑ I try to make my child feel guilty about spending time with their other parent.
- ❑ I try to manipulate my co-parent's time with our kids.
- ❑ I say things to my child like, "He never wanted to spend time with you when we were married. I have no idea what has changed all of a sudden."
- ❑ I say negative things to my friends and family about my child's other parent with my child present.

Ask yourself, "Do I do any of these things to my child?"

Another type of bashing is very subtle and I believe it occurs in many families but is not recognized as "bashing" because it is more passive and controlled. It is more covert. This type of communication can be seriously destructive to your child because this is how they will learn to communicate. Also, when children hear you throw out negative cuts or digs about their other parent—that person they are part of and who is part of them—it creates a negative feeling inside of them. Some families do this almost unconsciously, so I ask you to take a conscious look and see if you do this covert type of communication. With this form of bashing you are not saying something directly negative, but making some type of negative comment. Examples of these comments are:

❑ Your dad always did waste money.
❑ There you go again, lying just like your father.
❑ Your father will never change.
❑ Your mother never could manage money.
❑ Glad you made something of your life, unlike your mother, thank God.
❑ I bet it feels good to be away from her negativity.
❑ I am so sorry your father is such a jerk.
❑ I can't believe she treats her own child, her own flesh and blood, this way.
❑ You are so negative, just like your mother. She taught you well.
❑ I bet you are glad you no longer have to eat that burger casserole mom makes.

How Your Negative Comments Harm Your Child

I remember very clearly what I was told as a child: *"If you don't have something nice to say, don't say it at all."* And quoting from a well-known source, the Bible, **"Do unto others** as you would have **them do unto you"** (Matt. 7:12).

Guess what parents? This rule now applies to you. This is crucial for you to follow now more than ever. Here's why—when you speak negatively about your child's other parent, your child feels that you are in effect speaking negatively about them.

You are bashing your child and their self-esteem every single time you bash their other parent.

Why is this true? Because your child loves this other person. They are physically and emotionally related to him or her or has a history with their other parent. They identify with their other parent on a physical and/or emotional level. What this means is that every time you lash out at their other parent, they feel that what you are saying applies to them, too. Your behavior directly effects your child's self-esteem.

If your child hears again and again how horrible their other parent is, this person who they are half of, over time, the child will begin to believe they are also bad. It also

> **"If you love your child, you will want your co-parent to be a great parent to your child."**

makes your child feel very sad inside to hear a person they love talking negatively about another person they love. This hinders their ability to feel they can freely love both of you. I can tell you for certain that hearing negative things about their other parent creates stress in your child. Children cannot separate themselves emotionally from their parents. Parents are the models children identify with. They rely on your positive love and support for their healthy development. If you are saying negative things about their other parent (or any caregiver), who they rely on for love and support, you will negatively impact their development. Your child feels safe when both parents are there for them and provide a safe and secure environment. If they hear bad things about one parent, this will undermine their ability to feel safe and secure as a child.

I was recently working with a 7-year-old girl whose parents were divorced and still chronically fighting. Mom had recently had a fight with dad and had been gone for three weeks. I could tell this was very upsetting to this little girl and was part of the reason her grandpa had brought her in to see me. She said to me, with the saddest, brown, puppy-dog eyes and with her lips pursed trying not to cry: "My dad says [mom] does not care about me anymore." This little girl's heart was breaking. She loved her mother; she was part of her mother.

What her father had said to her was so hurtful and stressful to this little girl that she began acting out at school—no surprise. When a child witnesses his or her parents fighting and then is told one parent no longer cares about her, it is extremely upsetting, and those feelings often manifest externally as negative behaviors or physical illness. Research has proven again and again that all of these things are related. I told her that her mom was upset and sick right now but that her mom still really loved her. I also told her that her father was just angry at her mother and that, of course, her mother loved her and grandpa affirmed this statement. You could see a wave of relief wash over this little girl.

If you are a parent whose co-parent is absent, you may be thinking this parent-bashing behavior is not an issue for you or your child. Actually, it is. Shirley Thomas' book, *Parents Are Forever*, tells us that children can't adjust to chronic expressions of anger, blame and constant disapproval aimed at their other parent. When one parent is not in a child's life, this can create an emotional void, a feeling in them that something important is missing. It is still extremely detrimental to your child if you speak negatively of their other parent even when they are not involved in the child's life. Genetics and DNA are super powerful to children.

How To Break The Parent Basher Cycle

Life is too short to waste your energy bad-mouthing your co-parent. I assert that you should spend this energy taking care of yourself and your child. Every time you are thinking something negative to say about your child's other parent, tell yourself something positive. Let your negative feelings go. For every time you slip and make a negative statement about your child's other parent, my request is that you say two positives about the other parent.

1. Every time you think something negative about your child's other parent, in your mind think of something positive about yourself (e.g., I am a good parent. I am doing the best I can. I can do this. I love my child; I love myself. I am amazing).

2. For every negative comment you make about your child's other parent and your child hears it, make two positive comments about them to your child (e.g., your mom really loves you. Your dad is a great cook. Your mom keeps the house so nice). A few times of this should cure you really quickly of the negative, bashing comments.☺

Remember that your thoughts and beliefs create your reality. You actually have the power to paint your co-parent as a good or a bad person. I am guessing that some of your experiences with this person as a partner are contributing to your negative thinking towards them right now. Begin the process of seeing them as your child's other parent instead of as your ex-spouse that did you wrong. This person will very probably be in your life for a long time, and present (hopefully) for many of your child's life celebrations and milestones.

Consider how these events and celebrations will go. Begin in your mind to see this person as a good person, as someone who is easy to get along with and is a good co-parent for your child. It is in your best interest to do this. I am not saying this has to be true, I am saying that what we think, we begin to create. When we think or say to ourselves, "This will never work," the reality we are creating is that it won't or can't work. If we think or say, "I know this can work. I will do my best to make it work," we can then live into and create this possibility.

Exercise 4: I would like you now to imagine yourself working together as co-parents (not as a couple but as individuals working together to raise your child). Take a deep breath. Picture yourself at events where you are getting along. Life is easy. You have made the transition from a conflicted relationship to a calm existence. See yourself in a cooperative relationship with this person where you are both acting in the best interests of your child. You are focused on your child and their needs only, not your anger, fear or upset. What are the things you are doing to make this co-parenting relationship work? Say to yourself, "I can do this" and take another deep breath. Notice the feelings of peace and calm in your body. You have the ability to create this for yourself and your child.

Children Want A Connection With Their Parents And Caregivers

Let me share some interesting facts about children. From working with children from all types of difficult situations, I know most often children want to have a connection with both their parents. In some extreme cases of physical and sexual abuse, this may not be true, but it truly amazes me what parents do and their children still forgive them. To a child, each parent symbolizes a part of them. They want to have a relationship with each parent because these are the people who gave, or assisted in giving, them life and/or care in their early years.

If your child does not want to have a relationship with their other parent and there has been no extremely negative situation or abuse, it is important to ask yourself if your behavior is contributing to your child's feeling of not wanting to see their other parent. Talk with your child about their feelings and ask them what their reason is. It would also be a good idea to have your child talk with a therapist regarding this. It may be necessary to

"Children who were able to maintain post-divorce relationships with both parents were better able to adjust to the divorce."
—Mary Ann P. Koch, & Carol R. Lowery

have your child and their other parent meet with a therapist together if the other parent is willing. It is one of your jobs to help your child have a relationship with their other parent. This will promote your child's healthy growth and development.

I recently worked with a boy who would not see his mother. He did not like his mother's boyfriend or her relationship with him. My suggestion was that the mother take her son out to dinner at least once a week without the boyfriend. This boy will be healthier if he can have some type of one-on-one relationship with his mother.

A professional I respect very much recently said that if your daughter does not have a male role model/parent figure in her life, she will likely around the age of twelve seek out the first boy possible to try to fill that void. If children have a challenging relationship with their parent, they will likely have more challenges in intimate relationships. It is in your child's best interest tor them to have the healthiest relationship possible with their other parent.

I want to make a distinction—some primary caregivers may not be the biological parents of their children. If the caregiver assisted in keeping this child alive by feeding, sheltering or protecting them for an extended period of time, and they have developed a bond with the child, they are a caregiver of this child. In the mind of this child, this person is their parent or a very important caregiver. From this point forward, I will consider all types of primary caregivers (grandparents, relatives, etc.) who have done the work to raise a child to be of equal importance to biological parents. Whenever I reference *parent* in this book, I am also referring to primary caregivers that have raised or are raising a child. What this means is that if at some point in your child's life someone else assisted in raising your child, you must consider them as important as a parent and treat that person as parent to your child. Because of the child's bond with this other person, this is a very important relationship. These are usually cases where, for some reason, one biological parent has not been involved in raising the child. Someone else has stepped in for a period of time to be the child's primary caregiver.

You Truly Want Your Co-Parent To Be Successful As This Will Positively Impact Your Child's Physical And Emotional Health

There is something very crucial to understand here, if you truly love your child, you want your child's other parent to be the best possible parent they can be. You want your child to have some type of positive relationship with their other parent. Please read this again. You want your co-parent to be the best parent possible as this is directly related to the health of your child. If you are doing anything to negatively impact your co-parent (cutting them down, putting guilt on them), you are acting selfishly. You are not acting in the best interest of your child. It is in the best interests of children to have healthy relationships with their parents and primary caregivers, regardless of the relationship the parents and or caregivers might have with one another. Stepparents can also be very important role models for your child. My philosophy is that the more positive role models a child has in their lives, the better. I do encourage similar parenting philosophies when possible amongst the caregivers.

Having two committed parents through divorce and throughout life is a significant factor in your child's emotional and physical health.[5] If you can assist your co-parent in being a better parent, you have given your child a gift. For what you give, I promise, you will receive a happier, healthier child. Take the high road now to secure the best parenting by both parents. The pay off will be the future, positive relationship you build with your child and possibly your grandchildren, too.

This does not mean making excuses for or lying for your co-parent; you should be honest about the situation. If the co-parent does not show up for a scheduled visit or pick up, you can be honest and say, "It looks like you are frustrated that your dad/mom did not make their visit, do you want to talk about it?" You can also let them know that you love them very much. Remember, the success or failure of the other parent has a direct correlation to your child's feelings of success or failure— children don't separate themselves from their parents in their mind. If you truly love your child, you want their other parent to be successful. You will want and need to support a successful relationship between your child and their other parent for your child's sake. This does not mean you have to take care of your co-parent. Sometimes setting good boundaries with the co-parent can be the healthiest thing for you to do for all involved. Your goal is to create a healthy relationship with this other person, whatever that means for your situation. To understand what healthy is, you may want to work with a family therapist. Setting a good example for your child is the best thing you can do for them long term.

My Child Says Negative Things About Their Other Parent

So you may be asking: *What if my child complains about their other parent to me?* At this point, rejoice because your child feels comfortable talking to you. Your role is to listen to your child openly, empathize with them, not pass judgment on the other parent and help your child find the best solution possible. Approach this situation just as you would with any other concerns your child brings to you. Your role is not to run and call and yell at the other parent. If your child has told you something that relates to their safety or health, make sure to check in with the other parent regarding the issue calmly. I have learned there are always two versions to every story and you want to give your child's other parent the opportunity to share their version. There possibly could have been a misunderstanding.

When your child brings a concern to you about their other parent, your role is not to say negative things about the other parent to the child. Your role is to be a good parent to your child, which entails the following:

1. Asking them more about the problem, empathizing by making statements like, "That must be hard," without saying anything negative about the other parent.
2. Asking them what they think they should do.
3. Asking them if they can think of any other solutions.
4. If you have ideas, you could say, "I wonder what would happen if...."
5. If possible, the best solution is for you to help your child communicate their concerns directly to their other parent.

This approach teaches your child problem-solving and effective communication skills; skills they will use their entire life to be productive. Your job is to support your child in the problem-solving process. You are a resource for your child. This empowers your child and builds their self-esteem.

Question: My child's other parent was a terrible partner. Doesn't that imply they will be a terrible parent to my child?

Answer: NO! Just because your ex-spouse was not a good partner for you does NOT mean they will not be a good parent for your child.

What I have witnessed in my work with conflicting parents is their inability to separate this person that they feel wronged them in some way during their failed relationship, from the person who is now their co-parent. I continuously see these lines blurred when I work with families. Parents have a tendency to generalize that if someone was not a good partner for them, that they cannot be a good parent. It is crucial to separate your anger or experience with your co-parent from your ability to see them as a potentially good parent for your child. I use the previous diagram to make this concept clear.

The other important point to remember here is that you were 50% of that relationship at one time. Your beautiful child is a result of that relationship. The best thing you can do for your child is to create a new and healthy co-parenting relationship. This does not have to mean you and your former spouse have to become friends or anything close, but it does mean you will at least practice parallel parenting in the best interest of your child (parallel parenting will be discussed in a later chapter).

Joe's Story

Let me tell you the story of Joe. Joe was married to Jennifer for ten years. During their divorce, I worked as a counselor with their then 6-year-old son, Joseph. Joe said to me one day, "I know that Jennifer is a terrible mother, she was a rotten partner to me. After all the hurt she caused me with this divorce, there is no way she could be a good mother."

The reality I saw was that Jennifer was being a better parent to their son than Joe. She put her son's needs first and did not badmouth his father to Joseph. Joseph reported to me that he really enjoyed spending more time with his mom and that she had made a change. She was spending more time with her son than prior to his parents' divorce. He was really enjoying his time with his mom.

Unfortunately his father was jealous of this new relationship between his son and his son's mother. This was the destructive element of the whole situation. Parental jealousy is so harmful to children. Jealousy is a parent issue but inevitably children suffer when they have a jealous parent.

Exercise 5. Complete this exercise at a time when you are not with your child.

1. Do you ever find yourself thinking about the negative things your child's other parent did during your relationship when you are communicating with them or your child?

2. Do you ever feel jealous of your child's relationship with their other parent?

3. Could these negative feelings and thoughts be impacting your ability to see your co-parent as a good parent for your child?

4. Are you willing to let go of your anger and frustration with this person for not being the best partner for you, so you can see them as the best parent possible for your child?

5. I ask you now to write a list of all the things you are angry at your ex-partner for. If you make a long list, that is OK. We want it all out.

6. At the bottom of this list write "I choose to forgive my ex-partner for these things, so that I can see them as the best possible co-parent for my child. I know this will positively impact my child."

7. You may then want to tear up this sheet and/or burn it, symbolizing letting go of these hurts. If you feel like crying or being angry, please do, it is important to let these emotions out.

8. Now, to complete this exercise, say the statement below aloud:

My experience with my child's other parent as a partner is separate from their ability to effectively parent my child. I choose to let go of my anger at them and to forgive them. I agree to let go of any jealousy I am feeling about my child and their other parent's relationship. I commit to assist them in being the best possible parent for my child. I choose to see them as the parent of my child and not as my ex-partner. I choose to create a new and healthy relationship with my child's other parent.

Blurring The Lines Between Your Parents And Your Co-Parent

The next phenomenon that can be destructive to the co-parenting relationship is that parents sometimes blur the lines between their own parents and their co-parent. To make this clear, let's pick up Joe's story again.

Joe went on to say in our session, "Furthermore, Jennifer is just like my mother, always cheating on her husbands. My mother was never there for me, just like Jennifer is not there for me or our son."

Divorcing individuals sometimes hold onto old anger towards their parents and take that out on their child's other parent. Your former spouse may have some characteristics of your parents or caregivers, however, these characteristics should not impact your ability to see the other person as a good parent. Your ex-partner is not your parent. If you find yourself making these generalizations, this is a perfect opportunity to work with your therapist. Working with a therapist on this will bring you closer to working cooperatively with your co-parent to raise your child. Please complete the exercise below to see if this could be something that is important for you to look at. Even if you think this is not your issue, complete the next exercise anyway and see what happens.

Exercise 6

1. Do I ever compare my child's other parent to my own parents (i.e., he is just like my father; she is just like my mother)?
2. What are some of my concerns about my co-parent's parenting skills?
3. Do any of these concerns mirror qualities of my parent (take a deep look here)?
4. If you answered yes to either question one or three above, ask yourself this: How does this negatively impact my ability to see my child's other parent as a good parent?

Does this feeling negatively impact how I feel about them?

5. Now make a choice to separate in your mind your parent from your child's other parent. The more you can respect your child's other parent for his or her own good qualities, the better environment you will create for your child.

6. Now close your eyes and visualize your parent in your mind (you can do this with both parents if you want, just do it separately). Take a deep breath and visualize your child's other parent, now visualize a line being drawn between the two and say to yourself: "My child's other parent and my parent are two distinct and separate people. I chose a co-parent with good qualities."

7. List at least three good qualities about your co-parent.

1. _____

2. _____

3. _____

Be Responsible For Your Choices

This other person is in your and your child's life because of a choice you made at some point. My mom always said she chose my dad because she was desperate for anything after her dad died when she was a teenager. It seemed to me that in her mind, her father's death and her desperation excused her from being responsible for the choice she made in marrying my father.

Choose to be responsible, this does not mean you need to blame or punish yourself for your "wrong" choice. You made the best choice you could at the time with the knowledge and skills you had. Now, with the new knowledge and skills you have, you can make another choice—choose to be the best parent possible. If you choose to be responsible for the choice you made to be with this partner and to have a child or children with them, it will provide you freedom in your life. By accepting responsibility, instead of blaming your choice on anyone else or any other circumstance, you will be free to move on, to grow. Accept that you chose this person for a reason and, in the end, they were a teacher for you in some way. This may be challenging to understand but as you continue to read this book, it will make more sense.

So, you made a decision, whether it was your decision or the other party's to divorce (or separate if you were never married). You may even say, "It was due to all the fighting that we divorced." So, you made the choice to divorce, now make the choice to *stop* the fighting. Decide to stop saying negative things about your child's other parent. Remember again that every time you say something negative about your child's other parent, you are saying something negative about your own precious child. Make the choice to fully love your child. Choose to see the good in your child's other parent. This can feel extremely challenging, but I ask you to at least consider it—the payoff for you is a better relationship with your child and an easier life for you.

When you get angry at your ex, only about 10% of that anger is due to your current situation, over 90% stems from past hurts, and frustration over unfulfilled expectations. These past hurts can be from your child's other parent, your childhood or any other difficult experiences you have had in your life. It has been said that if you are hysterical, the cause is probably historical.[6]

You know each other's hot buttons. Think about it now, what makes your ex really angry? What could you do to really annoy them? Hot buttons are things that others do that make us really angry. This may include being late, not keeping things clean, or not paying bills on time (e.g., child support). Right now, make a commitment not to press your ex's hot buttons, it only causes frustration and anger. I do want to express here that I firmly believe no one *makes* us angry. We make a choice to *be* angry. So it is a choice if your co-parent tries to press your hot button. If you don't get angry, you win. And in time, when they don't get the angry reaction they were looking for, they will stop pressing the button.

If a parent feels the need to badmouth the other parent or to be angry with them, they are in a way just choosing to continue the relationship. This is called negative intimacy. They are not choosing to move on with their life, for whatever reason.

If you are in this place, you have not yet made the choice to heal and be accountable. I understand, this place can feel safer. It is scary to say to yourself, "I am accountable." If you can't be accountable for your choices, you may have to do some more work of your own. Ask yourself the following questions:

1. Do I blame someone else for the pain I am currently experiencing or the situation I am currently in?
2. Do I say to myself, "If only that had not happened, I would be happy."

These are two ways that you can avoid taking responsibility. If you have told yourself stories related to questions one or two above, it is now time to choose to let them go. Choosing to let go of the blame and taking responsibility

> "Every day you are alive is a chance to make better choices."
> —Bella Sebastian

for your life will allow your healing process to begin. It may be best to seek professional assistance for this. In this moment, you also can just choose to be responsible for your thoughts, actions and words. This does not mean judging yourself. It means being accountable to yourself and moving forward. We all make choices, some good, some bad. What is crucial is to choose to learn from them, and then make different, better choices, and move forward. This is healthy for you and your child. When you are healthy, your child is healthy.

What Your Child Wants Most Is To Freely Love Both Parents

This really seems like such a simple request but divorcing or separated parents can make this such a hard task for children. If your child can freely love both of you and know that they have good parents, they will be closer to loving themselves. They will have a better foundation provided to them from which to build love for themselves. This is so crucial for your child, I cannot stress this enough. Authors and mediators Elizabeth Hickey and Elizabeth Dalton tell us that children will not question their lovability if the relationship with both of their parents is fostered.[7]

Remember to avoid saying things to your child like, "That

(insert child's negative behavior here) is just like your father." This comment hurts your child at their core—it acknowledges their connection to their other parent while at the same time criticizes them for it. It does not assist them in creating a solid foundation. This comment impacts your child's self-esteem. It also impacts your child's ability to create positive self-worth. I like to think of children as being born with a beautiful bright light inside. Each time your child hears a negative comment about someone they love (or are biologically a part of), their light dims just a little until they are really upset inside. When your child is upset on the inside, they act out on the outside. Hearing these negative comments erodes away the vibrant self-love your child was born with. Comments such as these are born out of anger and resentment. One of the best quotes I've heard on anger/resentment is:

"Resentment is like taking your own poison and expecting the other person to die."
—Author unknown

Taking your own poison or giving this poison to your child is not healthy. We know from numerous studies that a great percentage of diseases are stress-related. Looking at the word disease, we can see dis-ease. When we are not at ease we are in stress, which impacts our health and the health of our child. It is your responsibility as a parent to be healthy for your child. Your child needs you—so let go of the bottle of poison and be healthy so you can attend to your child's needs. Especially the need of being able to love both parents.

An angry parent does not equal a good parent. I ask you to be healthy for your children. You won't regret it, I promise.

The Journey Of Leaving The Anger Behind And Loving Yourself

I know what a journey it truly is to love yourself because I still am on this journey. It has not been an easy road for me and if I can make this road easier for just one child, I will be able to leave this world feeling complete. At one point in my relationship turmoil, I decided I wanted to be healthy and have healthy relationships. Growing up in an environment of anger and conflict, I had so many unhealthy behaviors. I finally decided that I had to love me first before I could love anyone else. I realized I had to be healthy so that I could be a better partner one day and a much better mother when I had my own children. I realized that if I loved me, I would be able to raise children who loved themselves. I want my child's journey and your child's journey to be easier than mine was. Allow yourself and your child to have the easiest journey possible. That may mean accepting that if you do this, your child's other parent's journey will be easier as well. Who cares if that is a result, as long as your and your child's journeys are easier? You will be at peace knowing you did everything you could in the best interest of your child.

I am not going to tell you this journey will be easy. This journey of loving myself has been one of the most challenging I have embarked on. It meant I had to take responsibility for all my actions and all I had created in my life. It meant there was no more blaming others. As Dr. Wayne Dyer said: "No matter how much I protest, I am totally responsible for everything that happens to me in my life."

> **"No matter how much I protest, I am totally responsible for everything that happens to me in my life."**
> —Dr. Wayne Dyer

This journey truly also can be one of the most rewarding. The months following the ending of a serious relationship can be some of the most difficult in your life. I can tell you that on the other side of that pain is healing. This healing, if you choose it, will allow you to love you more so you can fully and completely love your children. There is no greater gift you can give them in this lifetime.

You will also be able to more fully love the next partner in your life, which is also very healthy for you and your children.

I truly believe forgiveness is a foundational step for creating self-love in your life and for teaching your children the importance self-love.

1. Are you willing to teach your child forgiveness by showing forgiveness to their other parent?
2. Is there anything else you need to forgive your child's other parent for?
3. What are you holding onto that you need to let go (i.e., anger, pain)?
4. Have you forgiven yourself so you can move forward?
5. How can you as a parent allow your child to freely love their other parent?

The Frustrated Parent: My Ex Never Wanted To Spend Time With Our Children When We Were Together

I hear this frustration from parents on a fairly regular basis. It is understandable that if your co-parent did not seem to want to spend time with your children prior to your divorce and they do now, it can feel frustrating. Now, they want to be an involved parent, which is what you wanted when you were together!

I ask you to please see this unexpected change in behavior as good news. The good news is that you chose a partner that is at least attempting to be a good parent to your children. This is excellent news for your children. Do not block your child's parent from spending time with them. Let go of your anger and jealousy and go out and have fun during this free time that you now have for yourself! If you do this, you will harbor less frustration. I can tell you that there are actual reasons for this change in your child's other parent's behavior. Let's discuss them.

The first reason is simple; when a marriage ends, it brings about change in individuals. Through this change, divorced people may develop new priorities, and come to realize that their children are now their family. The children become increasingly important to them. The non-custodial parent may especially miss the security of having a family and genuinely may want to be able to see their children as much as possible.

Honestly, this is a good change. It underlines that you made a good decision choosing your former partner, because they are now choosing to be a good parent through the divorce. They are not abandoning your children, as some non-custodial parents sometimes have. Research shows you will have healthier children as a result. This is good news, don't you agree?

The next reason for this change could be that you and your child's other parent may have argued so much that your child's other parent has distanced him or herself from the entire family as a result. So actually, the conflict with you could be part of the reason your ex did not spend as much time with your child before the divorce or separation. I am not saying I think this is OK, but that this viewpoint has been validated by research.[8] So now that you are not in the picture, your co-parent wants to spend more time with your children. It has simply become easier for them. There is no blame being placed here, just a statement of what is sometimes true. If you are feeling resentment, choose to let it go. Your family dynamic has changed and you can choose to focus on the positive—your child's other parent wants to spend time with them. This is healthy for your child, which is the good news for you.

When my parents divorced, both of these factors were at play. My parents fought continuously during their marriage yet my dad felt alone after the marriage ended. My sisters were nine and eleven at the time. The result for my sisters was that they were able to spend more fun, quality time with our dad than I did. He wanted to be involved in their lives. I was 21 when our parents divorced. My sisters have a closer relationship on some levels with our dad than I do. They took many long vacations during the summer together. This was very healthy for my sisters. Researchers studying this change in the family dynamic tell us over and over that the relationship children have with their parents is crucial to their future success in life.[9] My sisters both have healthy marriages. I am truly happy that they had this opportunity to spend time with our dad. Don't you want your children to have the easiest and happiest lives possible? If you do, it would be best for you to advocate for and nurture this time with your child's other parent and not to block it. Your children deserve every opportunity to have the best chance possible for a happy and successful future.

Ask yourself, "What am I doing to create a supportive environment for my child to love and spend time with their other parent?" What one thing you can do today to support your child's relationship with their other parent? This is critical to your success as a co-parent. Let go of your frustration with your co-parent, they are simply your business partner now— your business is raising healthy children. I know you want your child to thrive during and after this divorce/separation and this is a sure way to support them.

Exercise 8: How to Support Your Child's Relationship With Your Co-Parent

I promise that if you complete the exercise below you will be on your way to creating a better future for you and your child.

1. List two things that are good about your child's other parent.

2. Communicate these two things to your child. It truly makes children feel so good to hear one parent say positive things about their other parent, especially if there is a history of conflict.

3. Make a list with your child of the good things about mom or dad. This may seem challenging but just see what shifts for you, what space you can create.

4. Make a promise to yourself that you will not speak negatively about your child's other parent.

5. Take responsibility that you chose this person at one point, no excuses. No room here for self-judgment or blame. This is just what happened.

6. Forgive yourself. If this person was a bad person to you or not a fit for you, choose now to forgive yourself for: a.) choosing them, b.) the divorce or end of romantic partnership and c.) the pain your child has endured.

7. Choose to separate your own thoughts, emotions and experiences with your ex-partner from your child's parent's

role as a parent to your child.

8. Separate the actions of your child's other parent from the actions of your parents. They may act in some similar ways but they are not the same person.

9. You are no longer with this person, bottom line. It does not matter what happened any longer. What matters is making this situation as healthy as possible for you and your child. Make the choice to end the anger and fighting. Choose not to continue an unhealthy relationship with worse behavior. Set healthy boundaries with this person to end unhealthy patterns if necessary (more on this in future chapters). It can sometimes be challenging to see these unhealthy patterns if you are angry or frustrated. If you are still angry or frustrated, you probably have some unhealthy patterns.

10. Give your child the greatest gift of all—the ability to freely love their other parent.

11. Make the choice to heal so your child can heal. Your child's healing process will be so much longer if you choose not to heal. They will have to heal without you and that is a longer and more difficult journey for them.

12. Choose to allow your child to see their parent even if the other parent seems more involved now than they were before. Make this choice without saying negative things about your child's other parent to your child.

13. Do something kind for your child's other parent. Help your child get a birthday card or present for them. You can also be flexible with the schedule if the other parent needs it.

14. Thank yourself right now for reading this book and for putting your child first. You know you have what it takes to be a good co-parent for your child.

15. Remember you are human and you may make mistakes along the way.

   Because I love my child with all my heart, I choose:
   • To know and accept that I have a choice. I am making the choice to forgive.

- To forgive my child's other parent.
- To forgive my parents.
- To forgive myself for choosing this person at one point.
- To forgive myself for any mistakes I have made.
- Now to begin a healthy pattern of interaction with my child's other parent because this will ensure I am doing what I can to ensure my child's success during this time.
- Peace in my life, in my child's life, and in the world because children are the future of our world.

Questions For Reflection:

What is my greatest fear?

_____

_____

_____

_____

What can I do to lesson this fear?

_____

_____

_____

What support do I need in my life?

_____

_____

_____

_____

_____

_____

_____

_____

_____

_____

_____

_____

_____

~~3~~

Fatal Mistake #2: Turning Your Child Into Gumby

How Parents Put Their Children in the Middle

In my office, I have Gumby toys that I use when working with children of divorce.[10] One child I was working with had

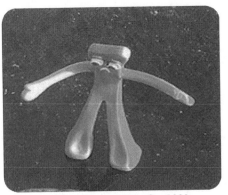

extreme anxiety. We discussed how children often feel put in the middle of their parents' divorce. I showed him the Gumby being pulled apart and asked him if he ever felt this way. He replied, "Yes, I feel that way a lot," with anger and sadness in his voice. Then as I held Gumby's arm in my hand, he grabbed Gumby's other arm and pulled on it so hard I thought it might break. The anger and frustration he expressed in his face and in his body as he pulled on Gumby was unforgettable.

You may be asking yourself, "What are some ways that parents put their child in the middle?" I'll share a few examples with you.

Stuck In The Middle of Child Support—Megan's Story

As I shared earlier in this book, when I was 22, the parents of the guy I was dating were divorcing. I actually think I literally stopped breathing for a few moments one day when

I heard his mom say to his 16-year-old sister, "Your father did not pay me your child support this month, so I am not allowing you to go see him unless he pays me." To fully understand the impact of this statement you must understand that Megan was supposed to be visiting her father at a beautiful lake cabin in northern Michigan. Her mom blamed this lake cabin for the demise of the marriage because Megan's dad had met his new girlfriend at the lake cabin the previous summer. The look of pain and sorrow on Megan's face was devastating. Megan was a child who chose to be silent and locked her pain deep inside. She did not say a word to her mother in protest.

These are the games parents play and, the children are the game pieces, being moved here and there with no consideration for their feelings and needs. Ask yourself:

1. Am I treating my child as a game piece in this Divorce Game?
2. If you are, how do you think this will impact your child in the long term?

Stuck In The Middle Of Parental Issues

My mom used to ask my sisters to remind our dad to pay his part of the car insurance or his child support. What do you really think this does for your child? When you ask this of a child, it puts them in a terrible position. You are asking them to deal with the disparaging remarks the other parent makes about you when your child asks them for the money, the insurance payment, or any other adult issues. This literally creates a feeling of hurt and upset in children's stomachs. This type of situation creates excessive anxiety that can lead to the physical manifestation of illness. Remember, this divorce was not the child's fault. Children do not choose this situation, parents do. So please be responsible for your own choices, be an adult and handle your own issue with your former spouse. Your child should never be your intermediary. They love both of you. Pay a mediator, if you have to, don't harm your child.

I used the word "stuck" in the past two headings for a reason. Children feel stuck or paralyzed when they are put in the middle of their parents' divorce. This can have long-term effects. Growing up with parents in conflict, I was always worried I would make the wrong choice. I felt paralyzed as a child. It wasn't until I traveled solo to Guatemala that I realized there really is no wrong choice. When children grow up in an environment of conflict and anger, they fear the repercussions of making a "wrong" choice. Your child also can feel so out of control, and may seek to control whatever they can in their life. Putting your child in the middle is a lose-lose situation for your child and you. It can lead them to feel helpless in their life.

Allowing Your Anger And Jealousy To Negatively Impact Your Children's Emotional And Physical Health

Jessica's Story

A few months after my parents divorced, my dad met his present wife. Well let me tell you, my mom was so angry and jealous, she told me once, "You are disowning me if you go with them." Whenever we were to go with my dad and his new girlfriend, my mother would make our lives a living hell. That is truly how it feels to your child. Statements like that put a child in a terrible situation.

My sister Jessica took care of my mom during this time. She was such a responsible child, too responsible. She also took on all of the stress of the fighting and anger that was still occurring months after the divorce. One night when I was home from college, I was sleeping in our basement near Jessica's room. I heard her get up in the middle of the night and throw up. The next morning I asked her about it and she explained to me that it was pretty common. I was frightened, I was afraid she might have stomach cancer. My dad and I took her to the doctor; I was so worried. After physically examining Jessica and performing tests that all turned out fine, the doctor asked, "Have you had a lot of stress in your life recently?" Thank goodness for doctors that ask those crucial questions. It was stress that was making Jessica ill. It was months after my parents officially divorced. They were still fighting like cats and dogs. Jessica had nothing physically wrong but she had a different kind of cancer all right. It was something I call divorce cancer, when the anger, sadness and pain of divorce stresses kids so much that they become physically ill from stress. If you are in conflict with your child's other parent, this conflict will manifest in your child. It may not be as obvious as my sister's stress-induced illness, but it is there. It also may take years to manifest. It may appear as a change in their behavior, as early drinking or drug abuse, early sexual behaviors, or poor school performance. Children who do these things are often trying to escape a stressful environment. If children do not feel supported and loved in their family, they will look for a replacement to fill the void. Kids who join gangs don't feel connected to their own families. They find the family and support they want and need elsewhere.

Based on my experience working with families, I can tell you that I have seen that conflict before, during and after divorce creates pain for your child and will have a negative impact on them in some way. Your child will find some way to cope, which may result in very unhealthy choices and behaviors.

Studies have shown that boys and girls from divorced homes and conflict show a higher incidence of physical ailments, including asthma, stomachache and other stress-related symptoms.[11] Parental conflict in the presence of children is also linked to psychological problems including: aggression, anxiety, depression, poor self-esteem, physical complaints and difficulty in school. Another child quoted in Long and Forehand's *Making Divorce Easier on Your Child* said:

> "My parents would fight all the time. It got so bad that I started to get stomachaches and felt like throwing up. My mom thought I had some sort of illness and took me to a bunch of doctors. There was nothing wrong with me; it was just the fighting really got to me."[12]

Recently, I read about a 10-year-old child whose parent's were in the middle of a terrible divorce. The book's author had interviewed the child due to parental allegations of abuse. The author revisited the child 2 weeks after their initial meeting, this time in the hospital after the child had surgery to remove cancer. The sobbing child said, "I need a rest. Can I stay here?"[13] I'm not saying that her cancer was directly related to her parents' divorce. What I can tell you is that this child preferred being in a hospital to being in the middle of her conflicting parents' divorce. She was crying out and clearly the stress was negatively impacting her life. Don't allow this to be your child. I know you love your child. If you are in conflict with your former partner, make the changes you know are necessary to end the conflict now and improve your child's environment, before it is too late.

Telling A Child Something Negative About Their Other Parent In Anger—Alex's Story

In one family I worked with, a mother adopted her husband's son when he was little. The parents had agreed that they would not tell their son that he was adopted by mom. Later, when the parents were divorcing, dad began to feel that his son was not bonding with him very well. He saw that his son and his ex-wife were building a closer relationship. So, guess what dad did? He broke the promise and told his son that mom was not his biological mother. Now, out of petty jealousy, his father added a whole lot of stress to a child who was already in pain. This type of behavior is irresponsible and selfish. If you make a choice like this, putting your feelings ahead of your child's needs, you are choosing to harm your child. If you ever do something out of anger at your child's other parent that impacts your child, it is wrong and hurtful to your child.

Triangulation: Talking Negatively About The Other Parent To Your Child

When you triangulate, you choose to talk negatively with your child about their other parent. Your child may even engage in this activity with you. This behavior is a very dysfunctional way to connect to your child and it will create future dysfunctional patterns for them in your relationship. I know I did this with my parents as a child. It was one of the ways I could feel close and connected to the parent I was with. If we talked negatively about the other parent, it felt like we had something in common. It also made me feel good, in a strange way, that they (the parent I was talking negatively with) loved me. It was also a way to avoid my parent's anger being taken out on me. As an adult, I still see this pattern in my family and sometimes I still find myself talking negatively about family members and relationship partners. It is sometimes how I connect to others, by telling them the bad things about others in my life. But I've learned that this is a very dysfunctional pattern to create in a family. Families are for love, not anger and fear. If you are a parent who tells your child many negative things about their other parent, over time this will reflect negatively on you. Children begin to realize that the person who is always being negative, is really the one causing the family's problems. It may take a while but this will happen. I counsel parents to "take the high road" and it will pay off for you in the end. Don't engage in negative discussion with your child about their other parent. Honestly, every time a parent says something negative about the other parent, this begins to actually reflect negatively on the parent that is being negative. The child stops hearing the criticism and just sees you being negative.

From my experience, it is my belief that if one person has to belittle or put down the other parent to their child or directly to the other parent, they are usually the person with the most personal work to do long term. This behavior possibly stems from their own guilt about how they have acted during the relationship/marriage and/or divorce process. This is just something to consider whether you are the parent exhibiting this behavior or are the parent on the receiving end of this behavior. Bottom line, this behavior negatively impacts your child. To help break this behavior, every time you say something negative about the other parent begin to think in your mind that you are saying something negative about your child. This is truly the truth for your child if they hear you saying these things. I do not believe that any parent wants to say negative things about their child. The bottom line is that your child is half of this other person. Begin to practice respect for this person, they are the parent of your child. You want them to be successful as this ensures your child's success. If you truly do not want your other parent to be successful, it would be a really good idea to work with a professional to understand the reason behind this feeling/behavior.

The Impact Of Anger And Negativity On Your Child

Remember that these behaviors negatively impact your child's self esteem. When your child is subject to hearing negativity about their other parent, it is like they are hearing it about themselves. In saying negative things or putting your child in the middle, your child does not feel empowered. This slowly but surely is chipping away at your child's self esteem. Is feeling right and bad-mouthing the other parent worth your child's self esteem? I hope not. Children who are repeatedly exposed to conflict can be frightened by the anger and this can either lead to them holding feelings in or acting out in anger. Both of these outcomes are not positive for your child's growth and development.[14]

Anger And Negative Intimacy

Anger and fighting is another way to continue what many experts call "negative intimacy." You have divorced or are divorcing but are continuing the marriage through this negative behavior. You are choosing to stay connected negatively to this person either because that is the way it was in the marriage or because you don't want to let go. This can create stress and physical illness for your children. One person I knew had lived separated from her spouse for a year and a half and they still were not divorced, even though her son's father had decided he was gay. When I asked her what was taking so long, she said they were stuck around money. I told her I did not believe that. I saw that money was only an excuse for them. They really were refusing to let go of something else. I asked her, "What do you need to let go of?"

I will ask you that same question. What do you need to let go of to move forward? Experts tell us that if you are feeling angry, you have not dealt with your grief. It is necessary to feel the pain and work through this event with a professional counselor.[15] If you are still angry, your children will have a very challenging time moving on after the divorce. Your anger keeps them stuck, too, which is not healthy for them.

 To see if you are stuck in anger/negative intimacy and refusing to heal, take the following quiz.

Answer *Yes* or *No* to each question:

- When explaining why you divorced, do you say your child's other parent was the main reason?   Y N

- Do you tell the other person they are to blame?   Y N

- Do you feel anger on a daily basis towards your child's other parent?   Y N

- Do you ever feel it would be best to get back together even though the other person does not want that or has moved on?   Y N

- Have you tried to get the other person to reconcile months after separating (and it did not work and you still want to be with this person)?   Y N

- Have you been separated for over a year and the divorce is still not final due to unresolved issues?   Y N

- Have you felt upset and angry for more than six months and have not yet seen a therapist?   Y N

If you answered *Yes* to any of the above, it could very well mean that you are choosing not to move forward. You deserve to move on with your life. Your child deserves to move on in life, too. Take whatever steps you know are necessary to do this. I have to add here that our family has just welcomed my sister's new baby son. My parents have done an excellent job of putting my sister and their first grandchild first. I am so grateful for this. The exercise below may assist with letting your anger go and putting your child first.

Exercise 10

Letting Go
1. Take a deep breath and close your eyes.
2. Take another deep breath and once you feel calm, ask yourself the following question:
Why am I not letting go of this person who no longer works for me in my life? Allow your answer to come from within.
3. Now ask yourself: What can I do or what do I need to tell myself to let go of this person or my anger at this person?
4. Now see yourself happy in the future once this person is no longer a part of your sadness or anger. What do you have, what is different, what life do you want to create? How will you feel in the future when you have this new life?
5. Ask yourself if there is anything else you need to do to move forward and out of the anger/sadness.
6. Now tell yourself that you have really done your best, or at least the best you could have done with the skills you had at the time.
7. Forgive yourself. Say to yourself, "I forgive you and I care about you, it is time to move forward."
8. Now open your eyes and write down anything important that you remember about this future you imagined.

Answers to #2 above could include: I'm afraid; I don't want to fail; I don't want to be alone; I can't be divorced.

Answers to #3 could include: Have a completion session where we complete this part of our relationship; just step forward and move on; know that I did all I could; know that my child will be OK and I will be OK; take care of myself, see a therapist.

Sharing Custody of Your Child

This may be one of the most challenging things you ever do in your life. You will have to relinquish control of your child to the person you may feel that you hate most in the world at this moment. During the time your child spends with their other parent, you don't really have a say in what happens unless life-threatening behavior is occurring. That means if your child's other parent wants to take them for a motorcycle ride and you never used to allow that, now they can. That means if the other parent wants to let them eat junk food, they can—unless you have chosen to create a cooperative parenting situation where you can decide together on rules and discipline. I advise parents that if theirs is an adversarial relationship, then they each really have no say in what the other parent does with their child—if you are not speaking to them, how could you? You do not have control of what your child does while in the care of the other parent. Your worry will not help your child or you. Let it go.

So, when your child spends time with their other parent, they will look for your reaction as they leave and when they return to you. Allow your child to go in peace and return in peace. Do not allow your fears and worries to create fear and worry in your child. Wish them a good time and when they return, ask how their time was. Let go and take the time apart from your child as time for yourself to enjoy. Do things you enjoy while they are gone. I wrote the poem *My Greatest Wish* that you can give to your child so they know you love them while they are with their other parent. It also tells your child that you give them your blessing and permission to fully love and enjoy their other parent. This will also remind them of you while they are with their other parent. They will feel secure in knowing you are OK with them going and that you love them. This is what your child needs.

My Greatest Wish

You are my child,
I will always love you.
You make me smile,
When I think of you.

Even when we are apart,
You are forever in my heart.
Know I am only a phone call away,
We are always connected by our love.

Think of me now,
Giving you the biggest hug of all.
I will love you forever, my beautiful child.
Enjoy your time with your other parent.

I will see you soon,
Until then, feel my love in your heart.
Be happy and have fun, my beautiful child,
This is my greatest wish for you.

I LOVE YOU, _____

Mom/Dad _____

How Parents Continue To Fight For And Demand Control: Forgetting That You Are A Co-Parent For Life

Let's discuss something divorcing and divorced parents sometimes forget. Because you made a choice to have children with this person, you will be forever connected to him or her. For good or for bad, in sickness or in health, you will continue to share a common bond with this person—your child. Your former relationship produced a miracle. Because you have a child together, your connection will take the form of sharing major events such as certain religious milestones, graduations, potential weddings and possible births of your grandchildren.

 Think for a minute of your daughter or son planning the seating assignments for their wedding. Do you want them to be able to not worry about their parents sitting at the same table?

If you want your child to be free to have a positive experience at these extremely important events, you will need to find a way to be civil with your child's other parent. You do not have to be friends with the other person, this is not a requirement in any way. You just need to be able to be calm in their presence. My parents were actually able to sit by each other at my sister's wedding. I was at the wedding-party table, looked over and saw them sitting next to each other and I seriously almost fainted as a smile came across my face. I know what it took for them to do this. My family has come a long way. You are powerful and can do this. It takes two people to fight; find a way to bury the hatchet. If you choose to make every life event an issue or problem for your child by arguing with their other parent, not letting a new spouse attend, or just being angry in general, you are punishing your child for your failed relationship. They don't get to fully enjoy some of the most important events in their lives.

By Not Being A Healthy Co-Parent...

> *"...You are punishing your child for your choices in life and this truly is not fair to your child."*

If you continue to make things difficult for your child, you are putting your own needs, insecurities and issues first. At some point your child may decide to not have you present at their important events. It is time to make a choice to let the anger go or pay someone to assist you with this. If you love your child, you will not continue to create an adversarial environment for them. Your children did not ask to grow up in a divorced or unmarried family, so help them make the best of it. As a child of divorce, I know how this feels because it still occurs in my family. I worry how my parents will be once I have a child. But you know what, if they can't act decently, we will just not see them, it is quite simple. I will not expose my children to the same anger I had to deal with as a child. For my parents, it took 15 years for them to finally let go of some of their anger. Don't let it take that long for you. Choose now to be a healthy co-parent. Your entire family deserves it.

Read the following scenarios and decide if the parent's reaction is fair to their child. Is the parent putting their child's needs first?

1. Your child tells you they want to do every other week with you instead of breaking the parenting time up midweek and you say no, you would miss them too much....
2. Your child talks about your ex's new boyfriend and you tell them to not talk about this person....
3. Your child would like to have their other parent's new partner at an event and you object as it would upset you....

So, your child did not choose this situation. Your role as their parent is to put their needs first. Your job is to do all you can do to make this situation as easy for your child as possible. In the first scenario above, your child is saying this would make their life easier. Can you imagine switching homes midweek every week? While it may be hard for you initially, you will adjust.

In scenario two above, asking your child not to talk about their other parent's partner is shutting down a crucial line of communication. You want your child to be able to talk with you about this person. You do want to hear about the good things in your child's life. You also want your child to share with you anything that is not going so well in their life. You can even change the subject quickly once you know your child is safe. You do not need to probe for details, just be positive and listen. The bottom line is that you want to keep these lines of communication open with your child.

In scenario three, if your child has been with a parent's partner long enough to want this, you should at this point not be hanging on to old feelings for your co-parent. If you feel this way, it is an indication that you need to do more work to heal yourself. Your child has every right to enjoy having others in their life. You will ALWAYS be your child's mother or father, do not ever think anyone will ever take your place. Consider this a positive thing, that your co-parent has chosen someone that your child does enjoy having in their life. Again, the more positive role models in a child's life, the better. Since you are divorced, this is just a fact of life. See it as a fact and take the emotion out of it. I know this can feel challenging and it is important to put your child's needs first during this time.

Strategies For Effective And Healthy Co-Parenting

Strategy #1: Choose to Take The High Road

If there is one concept I hope will stay with you after reading this book, this one is close to the top of my list. In the co-parenting class I teach, parents say, "I am the one who always buys notebooks for my child." What I say is, if you are not able to civilly communicate about this, then take the high road. If notebooks (or pants, or shoes, or diapers) are worth a huge argument, then you are not willing to put your child's needs first. This anger is truly not about the notebook, the notebook represents your old unresolved issues and anger at this person. "Let the old anger go." Let the stuff go, it is not worth it.

 With your palm open and facing down, lift your arm as if you are pushing up towards the sky and say to yourself, "I now choose to take the high road." This is the adult option. Please make the effort to physically do this, it is important to take the high road on co-parenting issues when possible.

Strategy #2: Pick Your Battles

A previous manager of mine said to me, "Shannon, I have learned to pick my battles." She was indicating there are things she chose to ignore because it would be a huge uphill climb. Make sure that the issues you choose to bring to your ex's attention are really worth the amount of effort you may extend in arguing with them. Always assess the cost-benefit ratio of your actions. Make sure the cost of bringing the issue up will reap a big enough benefit.

Strategy #3: Don't Act In Anger

Give yourself some time to calm down so you can think clearly. Don't speak to your co-parent when you are angry. Ask yourself why this situation is so frustrating for you. What are you telling yourself about this situation that makes it so frustrating? Take your own time-out if you are feeling angry. Do something healthy to help yourself calm down. The good news is that you always have a choice in the choices you make.

Strategy #4: Don't Battle It Out In The Courts—Use Other Methods Whenever Possible

A therapist who I used to teach a "Co-Parenting Through Your Divorce" class with would tell parents that we only had one thing to say about battling it out in the courts. He told participants in the class, "You will end up frustrated and broke." If you choose to battle in the courts and you have children, you can be assured of one outcome, your children will lose. I have also heard many parents agree that you lose complete control once you have given the courts responsibility for the decisions you cannot make for your family. And there are many other options, such as mediation, collaborative team divorce, and parent coordination, which are much less adversarial. Please explore these options for the sake of your children.

If you are considering taking your divorce into the courts or if you already are in court, please take a moment now and assess why you truly are doing this. Do you think this is going to be better for your family in the long run? Or are you harboring old anger that you are hoping the courts will work out for you? Is this really about your child or deep down is it your issue with the other parent you are trying to have the courts work out. The legal process is very expensive. Don't waste your child's future education arguing your old wounds in court. This is not the way to peace. I have included two sample letters in the back of this book. One is from you to your co-parent. The other is from me to your co-parent. Take a few minutes to review these letters to see if they might assist you in working your situation out in peace, outside the court system, for the greatest good of everyone.

If you are considering going into or are currently in court regarding your child:
- List the reasons why you are going to court:

_____

_____

_____

And then, ask yourself these questions:
- Is any of this about my anger at my child's other parent?
- Have I really given this person a chance to see how they will parent my child?
- Do I want to lose control of the decisions made about my children (if you are not in court already)?
- Is this court battle worth the damage it may do to my children's emotional and physical health?
- Where can I meet my co-parent in the middle to try to resolve these issues together, through a mediator or a parenting coordinator so that we can all move forward?

You may be wondering at this point what a parenting coordinator does. Most states have a professional role of this type, and they may be called different names in each state. In this role, I use all my skills and training to assist parents to effectively work together for the greatest good of their child. A parenting coordinator by definition in the state of Colorado is:

*"A person with specific qualifications that can be appointed by the court or by agreement of the parties to resolve parenting disputes after your case has been concluded. You can agree to make the recommendations of a third person binding by jointly requesting the appointment of a **decision maker** whose decisions can be enforced by a court order."*

—CRS § 14-10-128.1

The parent coordinator, if used effectively, can facilitate choices and change to promote long-term healing and healthy co-parenting for your family. There is no price you can put on the impact of this for you and your children. It is definitely a role you should explore. It can save you money by keeping you out of the courts. When I am working as a parenting coordinator, I also view my role as getting the two parents to work together on their own. My goal is to work myself out of a job. I do this though education, coaching and psychology. A former client who was not speaking to her child's father when we started the process, is now effectively co-parenting and had the following to say about the process:

> *"Shannon has helped my ex-husband and I come to a successful resolution of many of our conflicts. She has helped me to make the best child-centered choices I could, thus protecting my child from the impact of my conflict. She has helped me feel at peace with the decisions that have been made. I am deeply grateful for all of her time, guidance and patience."*

As you can see, other alternatives can work, this couple had begun the court process when I began working with them. I also want to say that mom's attorney was very amenable to working together for the greatest good of the family. Other alternatives to going to court include: collaborative team divorce and mediation. If you can use any of these, I would recommend it for the long-term health of your family.

Strategy #5: Follow The Business-Meeting Guidelines Model

If you and your co-parent are able to meet or talk on the phone, use the following business-meeting guidelines for your conversations:

- No yelling.
- No saying bad words.
- One person talks at a time.
- Take a break if needed—either parent can call a timeout.
- No bringing up the past.
- No blaming.
- If it seems like you are not getting anywhere, ask for the meeting to end.
- Create any other guidelines you think would be helpful and agree to them prior to the meeting.

Sample meeting outline:

1. Have an agenda of items you both want to discuss. You can both share your items when you meet.

2. Have a picture of your child in front of you as you discuss. Remember this is about them, not you and your issues, anger or fears.
3. Focus on the present, don't bring up past, unrelated issues.
4. Envision this person as a co-worker with whom you must get along or you lose your job (as a parent).
5. See this meeting as you would any other business meeting.
6. Use the words *please* and *thank you* as much as possible.
7. Remember to use "I statements" and not blame the other person. Take responsibility.
8. If the meeting gets heated and you are feeling your frustration or anger rise over a level 3 or 4, call a timeout, use the restroom or take a break. See Anger Scale in the Appendix.
9. If it seems that you are not accomplishing anything and the frustration or anger level rises to a 5, adjourn the meeting and reschedule.

Strategy #6: Use The Problem-Solving Method When Co-Parenting Issues Arise

This six-step method is good for parents who have some ability to communicate already. If you are not communicating, use this model with a neutral third party present:
1. Make an appointment—the person with the concern should make the appointment.
2. Describe the problem—making "I statements" so as to not blame the other person. State how you think the problem is making your child's life or your life challenging.
   Example: I am feeling frustrated with pick up times because Suzy was upset yesterday when you were late. What can we do to ensure we are both on time?
3. The other parent responds—not with excuses but with reasons for this situation. Example: "I apologize for being late. I have a big project at work and it is close to the deadline right now."
4. The person with the problem suggests a solution to problem. Example: "Can you tell them you need to leave early on Fridays or should we change the pick-up time the next few weeks?"

5. Discussion—the other parent either agrees or disagrees with solution posed. If you can't come to an agreement, table it for the day. If you begin to argue, take a break or decide to discuss at another time (set the time).
6. Review—go over the solution that was decided on or what will happen next (i.e., will discuss again in two days after considering options).

Strategy #7: Follow General Communication Guidelines

- If you are not able to communicate verbally without conflict, use email and text as a means to communicate. This is actually much better for your child than anger and unhealthy boundaries. However, it is important to not act out in front of your child if you receive a text message that frustrates you.
- Keep a journal of what happens during your time with your child and share the journal with your co-parent as a method of communication instead of talking at exchanges.
- Share a common scheduler when possible. There are many online calendars and communication systems for families of divorce. Our Family Wizard is one of them.
- Use "I statements" instead of "You statements", sometimes called U-bombs, because "You statements" have a very negative effect on communication.

Strategy #8: Follow the Rules Of Engagement For Creating Healthy And Functional Boundaries

1. When visiting the other parent's home, especially relating to the pick-up and drop-off of children, be respectful. This process needs to be very clear. I remember that my father used to walk into my mom's house, which used to be his home, but was not any longer. This would drive her crazy.
2. Determine what type of access each parent has to the other parent's home at pick-up and drop-off times (i.e., can they come in and wait? Should they stay in the car and wait? Can they come to the door?). Get these expectations clear for both of you.

3. You must transition your intimate relationship and all of its woes and closeness aspects to a complete business relationship.

4. You understand that there must be boundaries in this new business relationship. This is not a place for extreme emotion, this is a workplace, the place where you will grow and develop your child. If conflict is still occurring, contact should be minimal. If there is a lot of negative emotion, contact should be limited to text messages and emails unless there is an emergency.

5. Parenting is now your job as a divorced parent. You cannot rely on your child's other parent for everyday shared parenting. They may not be available and you must learn to parent your child on your own now. If this is difficult for you, I recommend taking a class. There are many resources on and offline. Try www.loveandlogic.com to find a good parenting class. You can also find helpful resources at www.theparentstoolshop.com. Don't allow your child to suffer because you don't have good parenting skills.

6. You are not friends with your ex unless this is possible for the two of you. You don't need to discuss intimate and personal details, you are now divorced. This only continues the relationship for one or more parent, making it harder for you and your child to move on. Usually one person may still want intimacy whether they know it or not, if this is the case, being friends is not possible. Being friends with the underlying need of intimacy will always lead to some type of upset.

7. Communication must be very clear and email may be the best method to ensure everyone is on the same page regarding your child and logistics.

8. Communication should be limited to those things that are necessary to discuss about your child. When you have your child, unless there is an emergency, there really should be a no reason to contact your co-parent.

9. If possible, decide on a time once a month or once every other week where you will discuss any important issues regarding the child either on the phone or in a public place.

Know what you will discuss in this meeting and stick to the topic. Stay in the present and know that compromise is the key. If you can't agree on something, table it for a few days. If you still can't agree, use a mediator or parenting coordinator.

10. Remember, when it comes to your child and their parents agreeing, there never is a winner or loser. As long as parents can agree, your child will win.

The 2005 Wisconsin Inter-Professional Committee on Divorce's *Structured Co-Parenting Training* summarizes the conditions necessary for successful co-parenting:

1. Successful co-parents love their children:
   - This means that as a parent you put aside your personal needs and interests to do what is right for your child.
   - You also think about what your child's life will be like when they are older and want to do what is right now so they will have an easier life as an adult.
2. Successful co-parents separate problems of the spousal relationship from the responsibilities and tasks of parenting:
   - Co-parents can resent an affair or other relationship and still make parenting decisions with other parent.
   - Co-parents can keep the feelings and issues about how the marriage ended in a box away from the co-parent relationship.
3. Successful co-parents are honest with each other regarding children's issues:
   - Successful co-parents commit to being honest with each other as it relates to their children.
   - Successful co-parents talk honestly about children and do not engage in discussing non-child-related information—it is now none of your business.
4. Successful co-parents keep agreements:
   - Successful co-parents keep their promises to each other and their child.
   - Successful co-parents know breaking agreements leads to chaos.
5. Successful co-parents set and work toward goals for their children:

- First, set goals for your children—what environment or life do you want to create for your child of divorce?
- Second, make plans on how to accomplish those goals—parenting plans and parents agreeing on behavior with each other.
- Third, carry out the plans. Co-parents work at successful co-parenting so that their child is successful in life.

Strategy #10: Follow The Co-Parenting Job Description

I created this job description for the role of co-parent, as it is truly one of the most important jobs you will ever have in life. It is very important that you and your co-parent understand the requirements. You may not have had a job description when you started as a parent, but now as you take on this new role of a co-parent, I wanted you to be clear of the expectations ☺. I had always heard as a Human Resource manager that employees were frustrated when they did not have clear expectations. So, here you are.

Co-Parenting Job Description

Title:	Co-Parent				
Reports To:	Self, Child and Co-parent				
Job Family:	Working Together	**Level:**	Executive	**Status:**	Forever

Job Summary

This position is the most import role within the new family organization. It is instrumental in ensuring that the emotional and physical development of the child is maintained appropriately. This positive role serves the child to ensure they adjust in the best way possible to an event that was not their choice. It is essential that this role finds ways to communicate effectively with the other co-parent. This role understands the importance of both parents being involved in their child's life.

% Time Spent	Essential Duties and Responsibilities
30	Ensures child feels safe and secure and has all physical and emotional needs met. Helps child adjust by providing stability and consistency.
10	Communicates in the method agreed upon with the other parent regarding important life events for the child.
10	Refrains from communicating negatively about the other parent in front of the child.
10	Takes responsibility for their role in the end of the partnership with the other co-parent.
10	Ensures their emotional health by taking care of themselves through good self-care and stress-relieving activities.
10	Responsible for minimizing the impact of the divorce on the child. This is completed through focusing on the above activities.
5	Reads various texts to assist them in understanding their child and divorce. Required reading, *The 7 Fatal Mistakes Divorced and Separated Parents Make: Strategies for Raising Healthy Children of Divorce and Conflict.*
5	Communicates effectively and in a healthy manner with the other parent. If this is not possible, healthy boundaries are set and other means of communication are established (email, on-line systems, texts).
5	Puts their health first and makes healthy choices for themselves regarding exercise, nutrition, use of unhealthy substances and their own counseling.
5	Fosters a relationship with their child and their child's other parent. Does things to show respect and support for this relationship to their child.

Knowledge, Skills and Abilities

Knowledge of children's basic developmental needs.
Knowledge of how parents' behavior impacts their child in the divorce situation.
Knowledge of basic parenting skills obtained through a class or a book.

Work Environment:

Home of child.

If you implement the above strategies you will no longer be a parent basher. You will no longer make a Gumby out of your child. You will be an effective and healthy co-parent for your child. You will be giving your child the peaceful and loving environment they deserve. In this environment, your child can focus on their job—being a kid with the least worries possible.

Love is patient, love is kind.
It does not envy.
Love is never boastful, nor conceited,
nor rude; It is not self-seeking, nor
easily angered. It keeps no record of
wrongdoing. It does not delight in evil, but
rejoices in the truth. It always protects,
trusts, hopes, and preserves. There is
nothing love cannot face; There is no
limit to its faith, hope, and endurance. In
a word, there are three things that last
forever: faith, hope, and love; But the
greatest of them all is love.
—1 Corinthians 13:4-7

Questions For Reflection:

What can I do to make this situation better for my child?

_____

_____

What do I have to let go of to do this?

_____

_____

How can I focus on the future?

_____

_____

_____

_____

_____

_____

_____

_____

_____

_____

_____

_____

_____

_____

_____

_____

_____

_____

_____

_____

_____

_____

_____

_____

_____

_____

_____

_____

_____

_____

_____

_____

_____

_____

_____

_____

_____

_____

_____

_____

_____

_____

~~4~~

Fatal Mistake #3: Not Understanding The Impact Of Your Behavior On Your Child's Development And Growth

Negative Impact #1: Fighting, Fighting, Fighting—Do Not Allow Your Child To Be A Prisoner Or A Casualty Of War

Always remember you are a mirror for your child. They model your behavior. You are the person they will learn the most from in their life. They spend the first 18 years with you learning how to be successful in life. If all you demonstrate is fighting and conflict, this is all your children will learn. They learn no appropriate conflict-resolution skills. They will not learn how to functionally express their feelings and emotions in a healthy manner. Psychologist Rex Forehand at the University of Georgia found that children learn their parents' patterns of conflict. Children learn from their conflicting parents to deal with problems with verbal and physical aggression.[16] In my home growing up, the conflict felt non-stop. My parents lived in continuous fighting and anger without ever issuing an apology. When I went off to live at college, what do you think I created with my roommates? I created all that I had ever known, fighting and conflict. I could not get along with anyone I lived with. I cannot even explain to you in words the heartache and pain this caused me. All I wanted was to live in peace after all the fighting I had experienced at home, yet I had

> **"If parents continue to argue after the divorce, children are likely to suffer."**
> —Phillip M. Stahl, PhD

no idea how to live this way. I had never been taught the skills to effectively resolve conflict. I still gravitate towards just one good friend versus a whole group of people. The dynamics of many people together as friends can still overwhelm me. I was and am an amazing person, however, I did not know how to effectively live with anyone.

People don't really like people that don't get along with others. Do you want this pain for your children? I know you don't in your heart. Research has shown that as conflict in families increase, children's social skills decrease.[17] Guess what I also created in relationships with potential partners? You guessed it. I manifested a lot of anger and fighting, the only technique I had been taught to deal with my fear and pain in relationship. Children growing up in this type of environment do not developmentally progress in the same healthy way that their peers progress. They do not learn crucial life skills that will allow them to be successful adults. It has taken me years and a lot of money to learn these skills so I could create healthy relationships.

In Jones-Soderman and Quattrocchi's book, *How to Talk to Your Children About Divorce*, the authors tell us that the harm caused by divorce to your children is increased by the duration and intensity of the conflict between parents. They site the following as direct results from high conflict:

1. Children feel overwhelmed by parents' hostility;
2. A parent that is not able to focus on the needs of their child;
3. Loss of the children's connection with their parents;
4. Parents that are not able to communicate in the best interest of their child;
5. Children do not have role models to teach them how to navigate life.

Is the continuation of your conflict worth the risk of these negative effects on your child? Research also indicates that the intensity and frequency of

> **"If parents settle differences and become happier and more content, they can do a more effective job of parenting."**
> —Phillip M. Stahl, PhD

parent conflict, the style of conflict, it's manner of resolution and the presence of buffers to lesson the effects of high conflict are the most important predictors of child adjustment.[18]

So, I completely understand and to some degree agree with parents who say to me, "I ended this marriage because there was too much fighting. I did not want my kids to grow up in that." It has been recognized by many researchers that a conflict-ridden marriage can be more devastating emotionally to a child than a divorce. Children are at extreme risk in a family environment comprised of extreme conflict, pain and anger.[19] I agree with this.

What I completely do not support is continuation of the fighting once the divorce is complete. If you divorced due to conflict and your child, then you are making a choice to harm your child even further if you choose to continue the fighting after the divorce. This is a double stressor for your children, divorce and conflict. You made a choice to divorce, draw a line in the sand and stand for yourself and your children. Make the choice to stop the fighting. It takes two people to fight. You have the power to stop it. If you continue to fight, it wreaks havoc on your children. Continuing to fight after your divorce is complete is possibly more detrimental to your children than the fighting prior to the divorce. Now they have to deal with the stress of fighting parents on top of a divorce that they did not choose. They also have to deal with the fear and insecurity that your conflict brings up when they hear the two people they love the most fighting. Seeing two people they love and rely on openly hate each other is so damaging for children. The fear and insecurity this situation causes does not allow children to develop effectively. They are not able to focus on the things children their age should be focused on because they are distracted by your fighting and anger. I have had children I work with tell me that their parents fight more now after the divorce or separation.

Exercise 15: *Assess Conflict Level Before Separation/Divorce, Currently, and Future*

Assess your conflict level on a scale of 1–10 at the following points in time by circling the number on the scale below (1 = very low or no conflict; 10 = very high or always in conflict).

• Level of conflict *before* the divorce/separation:

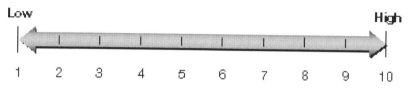

• Level of conflict now:

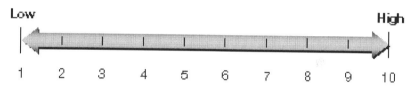

• Desired *future* level of Conflict (remember the divorce is your opportunity to do things differently if they had not been optimal in the past):

It is time to lay down the weapons you are aiming at your co-parent. This is important so you do not harm your child in the crossfire. What weapons are you still holding? Weapons that hurt your child can be anger, withholding visitation, child support arguments, old hurts, and small issues you continue to bring up. We have enough war in this world, let's not have war in our homes. You have direct control over this war.[20] Take control and make peace for your child.

Continued fighting is your inability to let go of this relationship emotionally. Make a choice to emotionally let all of this old anger that you no longer need to hold on to. Do not bring this anger into the new life you are creating for you and your child. Do this for your child. They deserve a peaceful life. If you are still fighting, you have not let go of this relationship on an emotional level. You must either make the conscious choice to let it go or seek professional assistance to do this.

At this point, I would like to discuss three types of parenting: cooperative, parallel and conflicted. All parenting communication fits into one of these three categories. I would like you to read through the categories and assess where you were prior to your divorce/separation, where you are currently and where you would like to be in the future as a co-parent for your child.

Three Types of Co-Parenting

Cooperative: Parents communicate effectively regarding their child's needs. They usually can agree to some extent on common rules and routines for the children. Focus is on the child and their needs. Parents put aside anger and disagreement to act in the best interest of their child. Parents get along well overall. Children do well in this environment and learn that conflict can be handled effectively.

Parallel: Parents co-parent their child together without a lot of fighting. They do this by not having a lot of verbal communication. They do not actually get along that well but they work together enough to ensure they are doing what is best for their child. They have been able to emotionally disengage and focus on their own lives. They parent in a parallel fashion, communicating only about the child and the child's needs. This style may develop after parents have been conflicting and are able to disengage from the conflict by setting boundaries and developing new ways of communication (text, email). Research has shown that this method is not harmful to your child. It keeps your child protected from conflict. While this option is less optimal than cooperative, your child can thrive in this model especially when there is healthy parenting in each of the homes.[21]

Conflicted: Parents argue and have anger with each other. Usually the child is put in the middle and has heard the parents fight on a regular basis. Parents are not acting in the best interest of their child. Parents usually have not chosen to heal their own pain. They choose to blame the other parent. Parents do not get along well and the child is impacted. These parents are continuing the fighting of the marriage, fighting over parenting styles, not willing to accept the end of the relationship, are jealous of a new relationship, or are going through a court battle. This parenting style has proven again and again to be detrimental to your child.

Children whose parents are in conflict prior to and after their divorce, do not learn skills to allow them to easily be involved in healthy relationships. They are usually developmentally behind their peers in the area of social skills. They probably will have a lot of work to do to be successful and happy in life. What we know is that when children are worried due to conflict, they become focused on survival and they hold on tight to survive and do not venture forth in life.[22]

It is crucial to assess your parenting style before and after your separation/divorce because it greatly impacts your child. This will have a positive or negative impact, it will be your choice.

Exercise 16: *Impact of Communication Style (Before Divorce/Separation, Current, And Future) on Your Child*

1. After reading the previous definitions of communication style, insert your communication style (conflicted, parallel or cooperative) at the following points in time:

- My communication style (conflicted, parallel or cooperative) before the divorce/separation:

   _____

- My communication style (conflicted, parallel or cooperative) after the divorce/separation:

   _____

- My desired future communication style is:

   _____

2. Now go to the following table to determine where your before- and after-divorce communication styles intersect. (Example: If you are cooperative *before* your divorce and you are conflicted *after* your divorce, you would fall in Box A). Use the key following the table to determine your child's Stress Level (SL), Risk to Emotional and Physical Health (RE&PH), and Future Relationship Success (FRS).

3. Once you know the letter of your box (A-I), go to the next section entitled *Overall Impact of Communication Style on Child* to read further information about how you are impacting your child.

Impact of Parental Communication Style On Children:

		Conflicted	Parallel	Cooperative
Before Separation/Divorce (BD)	*Cooperative*	**A** SL=High RE&PH=High FRS=Moderate	**D** SL=Moderate/High RE&PH=Moderate FRS=Moderate/High	**G** SL=Low/Moderate RE&PH=Low FRS=High
	Parallel	**B** SL=High RE&PH=High FRS=Moderate/Low	**E** SL=Low RE&PH=Moderate/Low FRS=Moderate	**H** SL=Low RE&PH=Low/Moderate FRS=Moderate/High
	Conflicted	**C** SL=High RE&PH=High FRS=Low	**F** SL=Moderate/Low RE&PH=Moderate/Low FRS=Low/Moderate	**I** SL=Low RE&PH=Low FRS=Moderate

After Separation/Divorce (AD)

Key

Stress Level of Child (SL):
High (least desirable), Low (most desirable)
- Overall stress that communicating this way prior to and after the separation/divorce would create in your child.

Potential Risk to Emotional and Physical Health of Child (RE&PH):
High (least desirable), Low (most desirable)
- This is the potential risk you are putting your child under with the type of communication you are choosing to exhibit with their other parent.

Predicted Future Relationship Success of Child (FRS):
High (most desirable), Low (least desirable)
- This is the probability that your child will be able to develop healthy relationships with friends (as a child), colleagues (as an young adult and adult) and future partners and family members (as a child, young adult and adult).

Overall Impact Of Communication Style On Child

A. Before Divorce (BD)=Cooperative, After Divorce (AD)=Conflicted:
Stress Level (SL)=High
Risk to Emotional and Physical Health (RE&PH)=High
Future Relationship Success (FRS)=Moderate

Summary: Future relationship success depends on age of child, on amount of positive modeling prior to divorce, or by future parent relationships. Emotional and physical health are compromised by conflict.

B. BD=Parallel, AD=Conflicted:
Stress Level (SL)=High
Risk to Emotional and Physical Health (RE&PH)=High
Future Relationship Success (FRS)=Moderate/Low

Summary: Health of child compromised due to fighting after divorce. Future relationship success will be low to moderate unless they see good modeling by parents in new relationships or others. This negative change is stressful for children.

C. BD=Conflicted, AD=Conflicted:
Stress Level (SL)=High

Risk to Emotional and Physical Health (RE&PH)=High
Future Relationship Success (FRS)=Low

Summary: No modeling of healthy communication skills, highest risk for unhealthy future relationships, stress level continues, developmentally challenging for children.

D. BD=Cooperative, AD=Parallel:
Stress Level (SL)=Moderate/High
Risk to Emotional and Physical Health (RE&PH)=Moderate
Future Relationship Success (FRS)=Moderate/High

Summary: Divorce is seen as a negative influence, less communication modeling. Parallel parenting works for children long term, once children adjust to change in communication. Future relationship success will be determined by the modeling children see and the age they were at the time of divorce. The older they are at time of divorce, higher the relationship success.

E. BD=Parallel, AD=Parallel:

Stress Level (SL)=Low
Risk to Emotional and Physical Health (RE&PH)=Moderate/
Low
Future Relationship Success (FRS)=Moderate

Summary: Children don't learn a lot of effective communication skills, but they also are not in the middle of fighting and learning bad habits. Easy transition for child, neither positive modeling nor negative.

F. BD=Conflicted, AD=Parallel:
Stress Level (SL)=Moderate/Low
Risk to Emotional and Physical Health (RE&PH)=Moderate/
Low
Future Relationship Success (FRS)=Low/Moderate

Summary: Moderate stress for child, modeling not optimal but not negative, average development of social skills. Depends upon age when divorced and how much negative conflict child saw prior to divorce. Also varies on the relationships child sees after divorce (new parent relationships and family).

G. BD=Cooperative, AD=Cooperative:

Stress Level (SL)=Low/Moderate

Risk to Emotional and Physical Health (RE&PH)=Low

Future Relationship Success (FRS)=High

Summary: Healthy children, healthy development, and healthy relationships. Stress is low to moderate due to change in family status which may cause child some stress initially after divorce.

H. BD=Parallel, AD=Cooperative:

Stress Level (SL)=Low

Risk to Emotional and Physical Health (RE&PH)=Low/Moderate

Predicted Future Relationship Success (FRS)=Moderate/High

Summary: Positive environment for child overall after divorce, can learn good communication depending on age at time of divorce. Future relationships can be successful depending on age at time of divorce and other role models.

I. BD=Conflicted, AD=Cooperative:

Stress Level (SL)=Low

Risk to Emotional and Physical Health (RE&PH)=Low

Future Relationship Success (FRS)=Moderate

Summary: Child will experience a decrease in stress and learn to develop healthier communication skills. Future relationship success will depend on age and modeling by adults.

The Good News About The Communications Style Table

Do you know what the very best thing about this table is? You have the ability to control what your child experiences at this point in time. ***Thus, you have the ability to impact your child's future***. Even if your child's other parent is not cooperative, you do not have to engage in fighting. Philip Stahl, PhD, a psychologist specializing in high-conflict divorce, shares in his book *Parenting After Divorce*, that the best way to win an argument is not to participate in it! You can learn good relationship skills and model

> **"I have found that either parent—by her or his own actions— can actually prevent about 75% to 85% of the conflict."**
> —Philip M. Stahl, PhD

those to your children. The healthier you are as a parent, the healthier your children will be.

Give your child a chance to succeed and choose a parallel parenting strategy. Studies have shown that children will be OK with parallel co-parenting. The impact of parallel parenting is not negative. With this type of co-parenting, parents are not modeling positive behavior but they are also not modeling bad behavior either. If you have a new partner, you can also make the choice to find resources to assist the two of you in having a cooperative relationship. This also sets a healthy example for your child to learn from. What I can tell you is that if you've had a past partner where conflict was high, it is very probable that you will need to do some of your own work to ensure you do not recreate this pattern with your next partner. Living in this type of conflicted environment can be extremely damaging for your child. If you don't do some work, your pattern of conflict is likely to repeat.

Special Consideration For Parents Who Had Cooperative Communication Prior To Divorce/Separation

If you were cooperative parents prior to divorcing and your children hardly ever saw you fight, you have a bigger job. It will be more important for you to ensure that you continue this cooperative parenting or at least parallel parenting after the divorce. If you begin to fight during and after the divorce, this will be a great stress on your children because they have never had to deal with this prior to the divorce. These children can be at the highest risk for at-risk behaviors and physical and emotional stress. The children of low-conflict marriages can be worse off after divorce because the divorce is the first serious problem they have had to deal with in their parent's relationship.[23]

> **"The amount parents argue after divorce strongly, negatively affects a child's adjustment."**
> —Dr. Nicolas Long, University of Kansas Medical Center

Moving Your Communication Style From Conflicted To Parallel

You may be wondering, how can I move my parenting skills from conflicted to parallel? The big-picture secret is to limit your in-person and phone verbal communication with each other. You must set boundaries so that you are not continuing the fighting and negative intimacy. You must move the relationship to business-like contact. Each person's situation will be different, but here are some general guidelines that may work for your family:

1. Agree on your child's schedule (hire a mediator or parenting coordinator if you have to so you can get this settled). My recommendation is, as long as your child is old enough, to do one week on and one week off. This arrangement minimizes your amount of contact with your co-parent. Again, this will vary by child, but I generally recommend school age as old enough to go one week away. You can also consider a Wednesday dinner with their other parent during that parent's off week.

2. In order to move your conflicted-parenting style to parallel parenting, you will need to have less flexibility in your schedules. There should be clear and consistent rules and structure to the routine so that there is no confusion and less opportunity for conflict.

3. A very common trend is to do "first right of refusal" for childcare decisions. This means that if one parent needs childcare, they must ask the other parent if they are available first before asking anyone else. If you have high conflict, I recommend waiting to do this until you can get your level of conflict lower. If every time either parent asks their co-parent to watch the child there is conflict, this will not be healthy for your child. Sometimes frequent negative exchanges between co-parents can be a way to continue negative intimacy, which is not helpful for anyone. If there is high conflict in your co-parenting relationship, my recommendation is to wait a few months and then reevaluate your conflict level with a professional to see if a first right of refusal arrangement is appropriate for your family.

4. If your child attends daycare or school, use this as the transition place. One parent drops them off and the other parent picks them up at the end of the day. This should be the norm for high-conflict families.

5. If possible, each parent needs a phone with a keyboard so they can text message easily. This was recently a $70 investment for me. It is worth it to be able to easily text instead of having to talk directly to the other parent, risk fighting in front of your child, and continuing the negative intimacy. You could make this part of the divorce agreement, that each party can easily text on their phone. This way, your time talking to this person is limited while maintaining a vital, open line of communication. To be clear, because it can easily be misinterpreted, texting should be used only for short, easy communications. If you have something important to discuss with your co-parent, a different means of communication should be used. You can also use email or leave voice messages when you know the other parent won't be home.

6. Consider using a website where you can manage your child's schedule such as http://www.sharekids.org and www.ourfamilywizard.com.

7. Have a scheduled discussion once a month to discuss any important issues about your child (use a parenting coordinator or mediator for this meeting if you need to, it helps the communication to be more effective and more progress can be made).
   If you are not able to communicate with your co-parent but really want to move from conflicted to parallel parenting, work with a mediator and, if possible, agree on the following important items:
   • Bedtime during school;
   • Bedtime on the weekends;
   • Curfew (when that age);
   • Rules regarding staying overnight at friend's homes, especially as teenagers;
   • Swearing;

- Movies and video games (ratings, time limits per day and content);
- Dating rules and guidelines;
- Add your own, family-specific items here:

_____

_____

8. Start to think positively about your child's other parent. Envision the two of you being able to cooperate for the best interest of your child. Tell yourself this is possible. See section on "acting as if" below.
9. No matter what your thoughts are when you drop off your child prior to them visiting their other parent, tell them to have a good time and tell them that you will see them on the scheduled day.
10. When your child returns to you, ask them how their time was with their other parent and actually be positive about their answers.
11. Always ask yourself before you enter into any action with your co-parent, "Am I acting in the best interest of my child?"

Acting "As If" To Improve Communication

Research on high-conflict families of divorce has found that one of the best ways to assist parents in moving to a workable co-parenting relationship is to "act as if" your co-parent is the way you want them to be. This technique, called "fake it 'til you make it," allows you both to build new habits. You may not want to be nice to this person, but just do it anyway. It may not feel real at first but it actually creates the reality. Saying "Please" and "Thank you" to your co-parent can be very helpful. You can also acknowledge them for something that they did do well can help to build the relationship.

Exercise 17: Assessing Your Communication
1. Recall your last couple of conversations with your co-parent.
2. What was the tone of your conversation. On a scale of 1–10, with one being calm and cooperative and ten being

raging, fighting, and arguing, how would you rate your conversation:

1 2 3 4 5 6 7 8 9 10

3. List some irritating things your co-parent does in conversation (tone of voice, mannerisms, accusatory words, etc.):

_____

_____

_____

4. What co-parenting issues spark your anger (being late, discipline differences, etc.)?

_____

_____

_____

5. What can you do to calm or diffuse your own reactions (breathe, walk away, do not engage, take a break)?

_____

_____

_____

6. What do you do to upset or provoke the other parent (come on, you know their hot buttons)?

_____

_____

7. What are some of your blocks to effective co-parenting? Check all that apply to you.

❑ Blaming tone   ❑ Not listening

❑ Thinking negative thoughts   ❑ Jealous feelings
   about the other person

❑ Unrealistic expectations   ❑ Jumping to conclusions

❑ Bringing up past history or   ❑ Discussing personal
   mistakes   issues

❑ Wanting to reconcile

8. What can you do to move towards eliminating the issues above?

_____

_____

_____

9. What two steps that you know of or that you read in this book, can you take to move your communication lower on the 1–10 scale to more calm and cooperative?

1. _____

2. _____

(Adapted from Stephanie Marston's book, *The Divorced Parent: Success Strategies for Raising Your Children After Separation*, 1994)

Work Towards Effective Parenting Strategies With Your Child's Other Parent

Included in the appendix are two sample letters to help you communicate with your co-parent in the best interest of your child. One letter is a sample you may want to send to your co-parent if you are not communicating well regarding your child. The second letter is from me to your co-parenting partner explaining that you have just read this book and you want to establish better communication with them.

In my work, I facilitate this type of communication between divorced parents. I have facilitated parents' communication as a parenting coordinator and decision maker. I do this work face-to-face and over the phone. I talk with each parent separately to determine if I see a possibility in your ability to communicate in the best interest of your child and then I set up a meeting or three-way call for all parties. This parenting communication facilitation has proved to be very helpful for some families.

Negative Impact #2: Being Too Lenient And Allowing Your Child To Set The Rules

Kids of all ages need structure to feel safe and secure. This safety and security allows them to meet their basic needs, which then allows them to develop into healthy adults. As your child enters into their teenage years, there can be some pretty huge consequences that result from not setting clear structure and rules up to that point.

Recently, I was speaking with my now 24-year-old sister. She informed me, "Mom letting me do everything I wanted as a teenager was not right." When I was in my late 20s, I saw my younger sister manipulating the heck out of my parents, and my mom in particular. My sister worked my parents against each other to do pretty much whatever she wanted to do. My mom thought she was doing the best thing for my sister. My sister thought she was the luckiest child ever, she got her way a lot. I became wise to my sister and realized that she was smoking, drinking and probably engaging in promiscuous behavior at age 15. I realized my sister could easily become a statistic—killed in a car crash where she or a friend was driving drunk, or a single, teenage mother. I raised my concerns with our mom. My sister told me that she had been really mad at me then for talking to our mom about her risky behavior but later realized I was right.

Sometimes, when parents divorce, they want their child to like them the most. They can feel guilty about the divorce and want their child to be happy. So, during the separation and after the divorce, they allow their child to do basically what the child wants when the child is in their care. Parents may have a difficult time setting limits for their children. Mary Hetherington's research at the University of Virginia showed that six years after their parents' divorce, adolescents from divorced families were monitored less closely.[24] My sister understands now that it was unhealthy for her not to have structure as a teenager. Your children may not like it, but I suggest all parents follow the below guidelines.

Parental Guidelines For Keeping Your Children Safe And Secure

1. Meet all of your children's friends.
2. Meet all of your children's friends' parents.
3. Have phone numbers for everyone on a list at home.

4. Before your child spends any overnights, contact the parents where your child will be staying to confirm logistics and ensure children are planning on staying at that parent's home the entire time. Ask the parent to contact you in the case of any change of plans.

When you have no communication with your child's other parent, most often your child is in complete control. Is it healthy for your child to be in control? If you say yes, you are saying yes to at-risk behaviors and you are putting your child's health and welfare at risk. Honestly ask yourself now:

1. Am I letting my child do things I probably would not have allowed them to do prior to the divorce/separation?
2. Am I setting consistent and healthy rules, structures and boundaries for my child?
3. Am I more lenient with my child because I want my child to like me more?
4. Does my child have the master control because of my inability to communicate with their other parent?

If you answered *Yes* to any of the previous questions, you have some crucial decisions to make. What is destructive for your child during this time is to allow them to get away with behaviors that you know are not right. It is destructive to allow your child to have control over the relationship between you, your co-parent and them. My sister was able to work my parents against each other because they had no communication. When my sister did not like the answer she received from one parent, she would just go to the other parent to get what she wanted. Since my parents were not speaking, this was super simple. My sister is amazingly smart, just as your children are. When this occurs, your child is ruling you versus you as a parent setting the appropriate rules and boundaries.

 Ask yourself these questions about your communication with your child's other parent:
1. Is my current level of communication with my child's other parent in my child's best interest?
2. What is more important to me, my child's welfare and future or my need to be right with my ex?

3. What one thing can I do to improve the communication with my ex so that my child is better taken care of? (This can include setting your own boundaries and using a different form of communication. You can do any part of the suggestions above).
4. What structure do I know I need to provide to my child to ensure their safety and security?

I know that all parents truly love their children and if you discuss this topic with your co-parent, hopefully they will listen so you can work together. If you don't think this is possible, please ask your co-parent to read this chapter (if not the whole book). Respectfully ask your co-parent for a calm meeting to discuss your child and healthy rules, structures, and boundaries for your child.

If you happen to be the other parent reading this chapter at the encouragement of your co-parent, know that no matter what your frustration may be with your child's other parent, they love your child and they are reaching out to you from that common place of love to ensure your child is not negatively impacted by your divorce. Even if you still believe the other person is to blame for the situation, I ask you to set that aside and to act in the best interest of your child. Honestly, in the long term, it does not matter whose fault the divorce was, what matters is your child. What matters most is that you, as the parent, are acting in their best interest. I ask you from my heart, to talk to your co-parent regarding these important issues. I ask you to communicate so that your child does not go through what my sister did. If you are not communicating, your child is at risk. You are choosing to put your child at risk, which is avoidable. Choose to put down your anger with your former spouse for the sake of your child. You will never regret it because you will raise a healthier child.

If the two of you just don't believe this is possible on your own, please contact a family mediator or parenting coordinator to assist you. There are wonderful resources out there. What is more important, the truly small amount of money you will spend on this service or your child's future?

If this change has seemed to make parenting more difficult

for you, I recommend a good, natural-consequences-based parenting model called Love and Logic, www.loveandlogic.com. This model will guide you in holding your child accountable in a real-life, natural-consequences way. I believe this model truly makes parenting easier. It is a good balance of many approaches and provides good techniques and tools. It will also assist you in assessing your current parenting style so you will be able to see the pros and cons of how you are currently parenting your child. If you truly want your children to grow into successful adults, they deserve to have structure and rules that will allow them to learn the best life skills possible. This may take a bit of work on your part. The payoff will be worth every moment of time you spend. There are no real parent manuals, so be easy on yourself. We only know what we saw as children, and we must learn everything else. This can be the good or bad news for you! If you take the time to do it, it will only be good news for your children.

Negative Impact #3: Upside-Down Parenting

The other clinically defined parenting issue that forces children into being the adult is called upside-down parenting. This occurs when the child begins to act as a parent to their parent by taking care of the parent's needs. Children actually can take responsibility for parent's depression and moods. They sometimes are literally responsible for keeping their parents going and parents have remarked, "I may not have made it were it not for my child."[25] This creates a dynamic that is detrimental to your child. Children are called children for 18 years because they are growing and learning. The way human children learn to be productive, healthy and successful in the world is through the guidance of their parents. If a child spends their time care-taking a parent during their childhood years, the child will inevitably have developmental issues. I always explain it this way to parents, if your seven-year old does not get to be seven at the age of seven because they are care-taking one of their parents, one of two things occurs:

1. They remain seven-years old developmentally and socially, which causes issues for them in the future with friends and socialization (they get stuck here).
2. They have to come back and be seven-years old at some future age in their life because they missed being seven at the appropriate time.

Upside-down parenting occurs when a child, being so concerned about his or her parent's health and welfare, does not do the normal things a child their age should be doing. The child is so worried about their parent that they forget to focus on themselves and their development. Upside-down parenting also may be that a child is doing the things that their other parent used to do around the home (e.g., cooking, cleaning). This is an issue when they are doing chores that are not appropriate for their age (see the Age Appropriate Chores List in the Appendix). This can refer to the type or quantity of chores. If your child is spending time parenting you or their other parent or is taking care of too many things at home, then your child is not playing/interacting with friends, learning and growing. If they miss out on these activities, it can cause issues for them in the future.

My sister spent a lot of time caretaking my mom, she was always over responsible and acted like an adult. My sister also had a very challenging time with her friends. My mom depended on my sister for emotional support during difficult points of the divorce. This was detrimental to my sister's health and emotional development.

Exercise 19 Ask yourself the following questions (check all the boxes that apply):
- ❑ Is my child reassuring me that things will be OK?
- ❑ Does my child sacrifice their own fun to stay by my side?
- ❑ Do I ask my child for advice?
- ❑ Is my child doing chores and things they did not do prior to the divorce and which may not be appropriate for their age?

❑ Does my child spend time caretaking me and making me feel better on a regular or even semi-regular basis?

If you answered yes to any of the above, it is crucial to realize that you must stop using your child for these purposes and obtain support from others instead of your child.

What one action can I take to bring other methods of support into my life (groups, friends, church, family)?

_____

_____

Please read the following statement out loud to yourself:

Using my child to support me during this time is not fair to them. I am standing in the way of my child's healthy growth and development. I will find my own resources to support me through this process.

Negative Impact #4: Treating Your Child As Your Friend

Children Need You To Be A Parent, Not Their Friend

Some parents share intimate details of their life to their children after their separation or divorce. These can be details about their other parent, details of the divorce or financial details. Children do not need intimate details. When I say children, I mean anyone below age 18. They are children and telling them details is treating them as an adult. You may be hurting and need someone to talk to, but your child should not be that person. And, just so you know, your adult children don't enjoy hearing the details either. It still creates conflict inside, even when your child is an adult.

This type of communication with your children causes the following for your child:

1. They will feel put in the middle because inevitably the details will include their other parent.
2. They will experience mental and physical stress from hearing these details. Your children worry. Right now they have enough to worry about and they do not need added extra worries that should not be shared with them.

3. The safety and security that they need to appropriately develop will be compromised.

In *Parenting After Divorce*, Philip Stahl indicates that the signs of being a friend versus a responsible parent include:

1. Setting few limits.
2. Supporting play and instant gratification vs. responsible tasks a child needs to do.
3. Undermining of the other parent.

> **"What your children need most after a divorce is a parent who isn't afraid to be the boss, someone who is willing to set and maintain clearly defined limits."**
> —Stephanie Marston,
> *The Divorced Parent*

If you are doing these things, please take time to recognize the impact these behaviors are having on your child. A responsible parent does the following to ensure healthy growth and development of their child:

1. Sets limits;
2. Teaches self-responsibility to the child;
3. Respects the relationship with the other parent.
4. Allows their child to be a child, not a support for them.

Exercise 20: Read the following questions/statements and check all the boxes that apply to you:

- ❑ Have I told my child information about their other parent that they do not need to hear?
- ❑ Have I seen a look of worry on my child's face when I have told them something?
- ❑ Do I tell my child details about my dating/love life that I would normally share with a friend?
- ❑ Do I treat my child more as a friend than as a child who should not hear intimate details about their parent's life?
- ❑ Do I regularly tell my child my problems, worries or fears?
- ❑ Do I expect my child to do things with me that I really should be doing with friends?
- ❑ I do not have at least one or two friends with whom I regularly spend time.

If you checked any of the boxes above, take a few minutes now to write down what you will do to take action to ensure your child is allowed to be a child during this time.

_____

_____

_____

_____

Sharing Financial Details With Your Child

If you are treating your child as a child, you will choose NOT to share your financial details with your child. You will not share your worries and concerns about finances with your children. This is a worry that they do not need to take on. They already have enough to deal with. Do you expect your child to pay your bills? If you don't expect your child to pay your bills, then you should also not expect them to pay attention to your financial worries right now. You don't ask your child to pay your bills because they should not be expected at their age to be responsible for that. They do not have the skills. It would be absurd to ask them to help you pay your bills. The same goes for expecting your child to deal with adult financial issues and concerns. If you choose to share your financial issues with your child, you are directly and negatively impacting their development. When children worry about financial details, they become stressed and focus on this. This takes them away from focusing on the developmental tasks and growth they should be focusing on at their age. This fear adds to the many worries and insecurities they already have. This is a worry that you as a parent can control.

One eight-year-old boy I counseled knew details about what mom was doing with his dad's money that only an accountant or attorney should know. The parents were extremely wealthy but dad was very concerned about the family's finances. He chose to share these concerns with his son, sharing explicit details about what mom was doing with the money, including "stealing money from dad." It was obvious to me that this father had his own fears and concerns about not having enough money because this family was very wealthy.

The fears were unfounded. This child already had so many worries and fears, the last thing he needed to be involved in was his parents' battle over the family's finances. It can be especially damaging if you are spotlighting the other parent in a negative light, such as, "Your father is taking all the money. I am not sure we will have enough to live on and pay the bills." Statements and insinuations such as this trigger deep survival concerns for children. You must remember that in your child's mind, they depend on you for survival. They want you to survive. If your survival is threatened, so is theirs. Remember, children need their basic needs met to excel developmentally.

You may be thinking, the truth is that our finances have changed. You may not be able to do what you used to do. The truth is that you may need to change your spending patterns. You may need to change your lifestyle. The answer is honesty—be honest with your child without complaining or being negative or worrying. Ideas include:

- We need to watch our budget now. We have less money each month to work with. There are many low-cost things we can do.
- We cannot go to the movies (or insert other activity here) every week. We need to do that only once a month. We need to do something else because our budget is lower now.
- We have x dollars left for fun stuff, what do you want to do this week with that amount of money for fun?

There are many low-cost activities such as parks, walks, bike rides, camping and recreational centers. You and your family may need to be creative. Your child only needs to know about what will truly impact them regarding finances. It is also most beneficial for them if they can hear about it in a positive, non-blaming way. Do not allow your money issues to create stress for your child. Your child's main job right now is to be a child, not worry about your financial situation.

The negative impacts that were discussed on the preceding pages can all negatively effect your child's life. The following diagram depicts how this works.

Impact Of Parent Behavior On Children

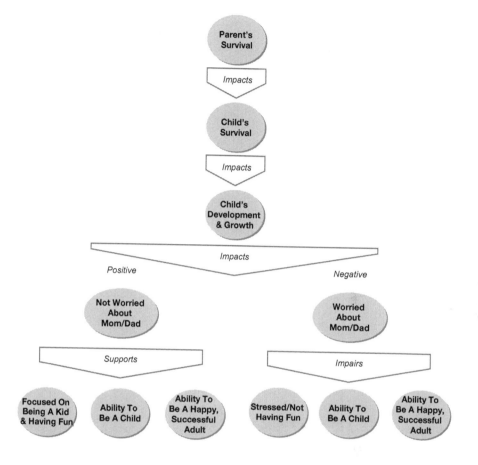

What Children Of Divorce Need In Order To Thrive In Life

This table shows what kids need from adults to thrive in their lives (adapted from Abraham Maslow's *Hierarchy of Needs*).

Child's Level I Survival Needs:	**Parent Focus On This First:** • Child has contact with both parents • Child is not concerned about your finances • Child has a safe environment, free of physical abuse • Child has safe environment, free of extreme conflict • Child knows where they will live and has a space of their own in each home • Child knows you love them (you tell them) • Child not asked to choose sides • Child knows where they will go to school and live
Level II Survival Needs:	**Parent Focus On This Second:** • Child has parents that at least parallel parent • Child receives parental support for their worries • Child only has to deal with childhood worries • Child does not hear negative things about the other parent • Child is nurtured by caregivers • Child gets to just be a child • Spends time with friends • Child does activities other children their age do • Has structure and age appropriate rules and guidelines • Has parents that can focus on their child's best interest • Child is protected from parental conflict • Sees a counselor • Child's relationship with each parent is fostered by the other parent • Parents include children in decision-making but parents make the final decisions
Outcome For Child (when Level I and II needs are met):	• Can be a good friend • Has fun in life • Positive self-esteem • Can work out conflicts with friends • Develops friendships • Physically and emotionally healthy • Excels in activities/sports

Long-Term Outcome For Adult (when Level I and II needs are met as a child):	• Choose stable and healthy partnerships • Love self • Commit to a long-term partner • Successful choice of career • Happy family • Beautiful relationship with parents • Physically and emotionally healthy

Negative Impact #5: Going To Court

I co-taught "Co-Parenting Through Your Divorce" with another therapist who liked to tell parents, "If you go to court, you will end up frustrated and broke." Fortunately there are many other means to deal with divorce-related conflict so we don't have to take our family battles into court. These options include: mediation, parenting coordination/decision-making, early neutral evaluation in the courts and collaborative team divorce. However, once you are in a court hearing there is only one goal, a winner and loser and in this game, your child can easily lose. Michael Oddenino, an attorney for the Children's Rights Council, says that navigating the court system as a family is like trying to drive in Los Angeles using a map of New York. I thought this was an excellent analogy. In his book, *Putting Kids First*, Oddenino states that all of his experience in divorce court led him to the conclusion that finding a good mediator (more commonly known in our court systems now as a Parenting Coordinator/Decision Maker) is the first step towards successful resolution of a custody dispute. Oddenino has witnessed firsthand that taking these issues into court is not beneficial for children.

I recently worked with a couple that had no trust in each other and were not working together for the best interest of their child. Taking their case to court was a definite possibility. This would have cost them so much money. More than that, it would have cost them any type of amicable relationship they may have been able to build in the best interest of their daughter. I believe that through the parenting-coordination process, we made just as much progress as they would have in court, it cost them substantially less money and they have a better relationship because they did not fight it out in court. It is a gift to their daughter that they now can be civil to each other and get along for her sake. When I do my work as a parenting coordinator it is for the future success of the children and their relationship with both of their parents.

The family court system in Denver, Colorado has an Office of Dispute Resolution that offers lower cost mediation to families. If you are looking into other less expensive alternatives, contacting your court may be an option for you. You may also want to consider collaborative team divorce which is a newer approach where all parties agree to work together and not take the issues to court. Court is not my area of expertise so I am not going to go into any more detail in this area. My final thought is that if at all possible, it will be in the best interest of your children to avoid letting the courts decide your families' fate.

Questions For Reflection:

What do I need to do to better take care of myself?

_____

_____

_____

What support do I need right now?

_____

_____

What can I do to promote my child's healthy growth and development?

_____

_____

Is my child's happiness worth me taking action in my life?

_____

_____

_____

_____

_____

_____

_____

_____

_____

_____

_____

_____

~~5~~

Fatal Mistake #4: Not Understanding The Needs Of Your Child

You can contest everything else, but one thing that we know to be true is your child did not choose this divorce. I believe that since this divorce or separation was the decision of adults, you have the responsibility to make this situation the easiest possible for your child. Sometimes, you may feel put out. I am here to tell you that your child feels put out a lot. It is important to realize how much your choices have impacted or will impact your child. Even if you feel that you did not choose this divorce/separation, you still chose this other person to have a child with. You must take responsibility and make this situation the best possible for your child. To do this, you must understand their needs.

> **"The best inheritance a parent can give to their children is a few minutes of their time each day."**
> —O.A. Battista

Misunderstood Need #1: Not Communicating/Connecting Enough With Your Child

Your child needs you to communicate with them. In the book *Difficult Questions Kids Ask and Are Afraid to Ask About Divorce*, authors Meg F. Schneider and Joan Zuckerberg state that divorce will be traumatic for kids if parents fail to communicate with their children.[26] Be aware of when your children need to talk with you. Make sure your child knows you are there for them verbally and physically. The authors indicate that when a child asks a question, be aware of what may be beneath that question or what your child really may be asking. Look deeper into your child's questions; make sure you are spending one-on-one time with your child, this is crucial. Ask your child how *they* are doing. Listen openly and with curiosity to your child, without judgment or opinion. Whenever your child is ready to talk, be ready to listen. If you don't connect with your child and listen to them, they will find *others* who will. These *others* may not be the best influences for your child, especially in the teenage years. Your child will seek the comfort and connection that they are missing with you from others, which can lead to underage drinking, teenage pregnancy and many other behaviors that have potentially life-changing consequences.

Ask Yourself, "Have I Connected To My Child Today?"

Connecting to your child and spending time alone with them is one of the most important things you can do for your child. In his book, *The Parents Book About Divorce*, Richard Gardner, M.D. discusses spending time alone with your child:

"Time alone with children is one of the most potent and preventative things you can do. One of the most effective cures for psychological disturbance is the parent spending time alone with each child."[27]

All children crave one-on-one time with their parents. This is so important to your children, it makes them feel special and loved. I advise parents to call this time "date night with the kids" or something similar. If you have more than one child, you can alternate each week who gets this one-on-one time with you. If it is the end of the day and you have not connected with your child, take time before bed to spend 5–10 minutes asking your child about their day. This 5–10 minutes has the potential over time to build a strong, life-long relationship with your child.

Guidelines For Connecting With Your Child: When They Are Upset Or Have A Concern

1. Put away any distractions so you can completely focus on

your child, shut off cell phone, move away from computer, put the meal on hold, do whatever is necessary to remove any distractions. Have your child do the same.

2. Take a deep breath so you are present with your child; clear your mind of other thoughts. Have an open heart and mind. Say to yourself, "I am here for my child."
3. Face your child squarely and be at their level. Sit on the floor with them if that is where they are.
4. Ask your child questions about what they have said, for example, "How does that make you feel?"
5. Empathize with your child. "Seems like you are feeling..." e.g., 'sad' or 'angry' or 'frustrated.' Or simply, "How are you feeling?" Don't put your opinions on them or assume they are feeling a certain way.
6. Ask your child questions about the issue and brainstorm solutions with them. Be sure you are listening to your child's issue and helping them solve the issue themselves.
7. At the end of your discussion, physically connect with your child to show them you love them. Give your child a hug or a pat on the back. You can also tell them verbally how much you love them. If appropriate, you can say how proud you are of them or how much confidence you have in them that they can make good choices.

Misunderstood Need #2: Not Having Your Child Work With A Professional

Some parents may feel bad that their child "has" to see a professional due to their divorce. You should only feel bad if you do **not** have your child see a professional. My model of working with families of divorce is a proactive model. I do not believe something has to be "wrong" with the child. Children need to process their divorce experience with a professional so that nothing stands in your child's way of living to their full potential. Even in the best divorce situations, children still have huge feelings; acknowledging these feelings early on is healthy. With every child I work with, I work through the child's concerns so they can let them go and move forward more easily in life. If they don't acknowledge them now, they will have to do this work later and it will be far more difficult for them later in life. Give your child the gift of working with someone who can assist them now in living to their full potential. I prefer to work with children early on vs. later when they are having bigger issues such as failing in school, drugs, drinking, etc. I talked with a counselor who saw teenage children for many different issues. Her practice was not focused on children of divorce, its focus was teens with issues. She said, "Most of the children I see are children of divorce. That ends up being a focus of my practice by default."

National studies report that children of divorce are referred for mental health visits about three times as often as children in two-parent, intact families.[28] Please note, these are not proactive visits, these are children with issues after the divorce has occurred. This is my point. If we take care of children up front, they will struggle less and have to seek less counseling later as teenagers or in their adult years.

Todd's Story

I want to share with you a case that illustrates my point. Todd, from age five to 13, believed that he caused his parents' divorce. When Todd was five, in the midst of one of his parents' many fights, his father said to him, "If you don't stop jumping on that bed, I am going to leave." That day Todd's dad left and never returned to the family home.

By age 13, Todd had been living believing he was the cause of his father's leaving for eight years and was dealing with depression. Finally a counselor told him that it was not true. By this point, the damage had been done and Todd was hospitalized for depression and suicidal thoughts a couple of years later. Todd was eventually diagnosed with bipolar disorder and post-traumatic stress disorder (PTSD). His PTSD was attributed to his parents' divorce. He is an amazing man and his path has been different as a result of some of the events in his life. Be clear, I am not saying that divorce causes mental health issues for children. I do not believe all cases are as extreme as Todd's, but children have different levels of resiliency. If you have two children, they usually will react differently to your divorce. I do not know for certain how your children will be impacted by your divorce. I ask you not to take the risk that your children will go through the struggles that Todd and many other children have endured. Have your child see a counselor early in the divorce process to identify and address their issues and questions.

You may be wondering why this is so crucial for children. Studies have shown that children who have proactively had professional counseling as part of their family's divorce process, believe the counseling helped them cope with the anxiety and stress related to the divorce. The next few paragraphs should help you understand why.

How Counseling Helps Kids

One-on-One Focused Time for Your Child: Spending time with a counselor provides your child with one-on-one time with an adult who is focused on them. This can be especially crucial if parents are struggling emotionally. When I work with children, we sometimes discuss and process difficult things. We also have fun together. I always spend some time with each child doing something that they enjoy doing. There is always time in my sessions where the child has complete control. Children can sometimes feel out of control during the divorce. Children thrive when they feel that they are the focus of the session and this is special time just for them.

Someone to Share Their Feelings With: Children can share with counselors what they may be afraid to share with their parents. Your children may not want to share certain things with you for various reasons. The biggest reason is that they do not want to hurt you or your feelings. They want to protect you. Children are so amazingly intelligent. They have so many amazing thoughts and concerns going through their minds. You would not believe some of the concerns I have heard. I would never believe them had I not heard them directly from the children as I worked with them. Children may be afraid to share these concerns with you. They also may have been asked to keep secrets by one or both of their parents. Once your child trusts their therapist, they can share these concerns with the therapist. I tell all the children I work with that they can tell me anything and I will not share it with their parents unless it is a life-threatening situation and I have to tell. I do tell them that if I think we should share it with their parents, that we will discuss this. This gives children a lot of freedom in being able to work with me to process some deep fears. I want children to trust me because my goal as a therapist is to be there for them. If they can share something with me, and choose not to share it with their parents, I still believe that it is healthier because the child and I can process through the concern. They are able to release a lot of stress in sharing their fear with me. This promotes healthy development for your child.

This does not mean that as a parent you have done anything wrong, it just means your child may have fears they feel they can't share with you. In one case, a little boy told me, "I know I did not cause the divorce but what I do know is that my parents started fighting more once I was born." So I said, "I will bet you a million bucks that if we ask your mom, she will say that was not true!" We had a deal. So we left my office and went to talk with his mom. The child was afraid to ask mom so I asked if it was OK if I asked mom and he said yes. Mom's reaction was, "Oh no, we were so happy when you arrived! We had been waiting for so long for you to come." The smile on this child's face almost lit the room. The relief on mom's face was worth a million dollars.

Children's fears relate to the unknown. Children need help sorting out what is real and what is not and what is true and what is not. Once children trust a counselor, they will sort these questions out with the counselor and get the relief that they need.

Child Feels Supported by Adult: Counseling is important for children because it allows them to feel completely supported during this time. Children feel that they have their own personal advocate who understands them, which is true. Many times I act as a mediator with parents and children, to help facilitate communication of worries and concerns. I assist parents to understand how they can better assist their child during this time. I recently worked with a teenage girl who expressed that she felt such a void at the end of her day because dad was no longer there when she came home from school. We decided to share this with her dad and asked him to call her more frequently in the evenings. This worked and was a win-win solution for both of them.

If Parents Are Fighting, Counseling Can Provide a Place of Refuge: I heard a parent pose the following scenario to an adult counselor. He indicated that he and his ex-wife were fighting terribly. He asked if they should get counseling for their children. The response from the counselor was, "Get help for you and your children will get better." I do agree with that statement *but* I believe a large piece was missing. I felt that we were selling out on the children. First, the truth is that some parents don't get better. Sometimes the fighting and pain continues for various reasons. If we can at least provide counseling support for the children, we can provide so much for them. Second, even if parents get counseling, their children will need someone as well. It is only fair for them to have their own focused time and process.

If you and your child's other parent are fighting, an emotional war is being simultaneously waged within your child. They need someone to help them make sense of this internal war, someone who can help them

"We were saying that we want to go to college and then set up a practice to work with children of divorce, like our counselor."

see they don't have to take sides in this divorce and that this divorce is not about them. Children know what is going on during this time, no matter how much you try to conceal your pain. Children become hypersensitive to everything during this time. Saying that your children do not need assistance as long as mom and dad have counseling is like saying your family's ship is sinking and, as long as mom and dad get on a life boat, the children on the sinking ship will be OK, too. Don't leave your children on the sinking ship. They need you to support them by finding an excellent professional for them to work with.

Just as you are figuring out the details of divorce with trained professionals (lawyers, mediators, and financial planners), your child needs to work with someone to assist them. This professional can help them take the easiest road possible through the quagmire of the divorce. We will discuss later how to look for the best professional possible

Please remember that even if your divorce is going well, your children will still have fears and concerns that they may need to work through with a professional. Sometimes children who have had cooperative married parents have the toughest time with the divorce because they completely did not expect it. A friend of mine shared her story with me when I began this work. She and her ex-husband had gone through an amicable divorce seven-years earlier. Because she was very aware and wanted her children to be healthy through the divorce, she decided to have her children see a counselor even though it was a good divorce overall, as far as divorces go. The kids attended counseling and everything went well. Her children are now 14- and 16-years old. She recently overheard them talking and asked what they were discussing. They told her, "We were saying that we want to go to college and then work with children of divorce, like our counselor." That statement is all the validation I need to know that the work I do as a counselor positively impacts children's lives.

There is so much research out there now on the negative impact of divorce on children that not seeing a counselor seems irresponsible to me. Recently, a mother told me, I am spending so much money on attorneys, I just can't afford for my child to see you. Wow, $220 per hour for an attorney (a cheap one), and $100 per hour for your child's future. This seems like such an easy choice. In the end, a counselor's bill is usually 1/10 of an attorney's fees. Know that an investment in your child now will pay off through their future mental and physical health as they grow. If you choose to take some of the advice in this book, you will probably pay enough less in attorney's fees to easily pay for counseling for your child. Make the choice that makes the most sense for your child. Allow your child to move through this time in the healthiest way possible.

When Should My Child See A Therapist?

1. As a proactive measure to ensure they are doing OK and to get their fears addressed by an objective person during the divorce so that these fears and concerns are less likely to turn into the behaviors listed in reason #3.
2. If you are in a lot of conflict with their other parent.
3. If your child is exhibiting one or more of the following symptoms and it seems to be getting worse or at least not getting any better:
   - Defiant and oppositional behavior
   - Angry outbursts of yelling, hitting or tantrums over small things
   - Sadness and withdrawal—child continues to grieve for other parent or the family
   - Issues with their friends—can't get along with friends or does not have friends
   - Academic problems—poor performance even after you have worked with teachers
   - Problems in their relationships with other adults
   - Promiscuous, harmful or non-legal behaviors such as smoking, stealing, cutting themselves, drinking, drugs or sexual acting out
4. Specific questions every parent should ask (developed by the U.S. Department of Human Services):

   Does My Child:
   - Often seem sad, tired, restless or out of sorts?   Y or N
   - Spend a lot of time alone?   Y or N
   - Have low self-esteem?   Y or N
   - Have trouble getting along with family, friends and peers?   Y or N
   - Have frequent outbursts of shouting, complaining or crying?   Y or N
   - Have trouble performing or behaving in school?   Y or N
   - Show sudden changes in eating patterns?   Y or N
   - Sleep too much or not enough?   Y or N
   - Have trouble paying attention or concentrating on tasks like homework?   Y or N

- Seem to have lost interest in hobbies
  like music or sports?   Y or N
- Show signs of using drugs/alcohol?   Y or N
- Talk about death or suicide? **   Y or N

If you answered *Yes* to four or more of these questions, and these behaviors last longer than 2 weeks, you should seek professional help for your child.[30]

Note** If your child mentions thoughts of harming themselves, you should contact a professional immediately.

What Might My Child Gain From Therapy?

- Increased self-esteem
- Improved coping skills
- Feelings will be expressed and validated
- Concerns addressed and let go of
- Stress reduction
- Sense of being in control in their life

What If My Child Does Not Want To Attend Therapy?

This is a concern I sometimes hear. Please remember you are the parent. Your job is to ensure your child has the necessary resources to grow into a healthy adult. You sometimes need to make these important decisions for your children. If you don't, you may not be acting in the best interest of your child. If this is a concern for parents, I say to them, bring your child in and if they don't want to return we can discuss that. I have never had a child not want to return. It is important to tell your therapist your child is feeling this way, because it will allow them to better design their first session with your child. Another method I use is to request that we hold three sessions and then everyone can talk and decide if it is best to continue at this time. Some children may not be ready and we cannot force those children to be ready. However, you should allow a trained therapist to assist you in making that decision.

The decision to have your child see a therapist can be a challenging one. There are now many professionals who specialize in children and divorce. To assist you in choosing the best therapist possible for your child, here are some questions to ask a potential therapist *prior* to telling them about your personal situation:

Questions To Ask Potential Therapists (And Why)

1. What is the focus of your practice? Do you work with adults, children or both? If both, what percentage of your practice is children? (If this person specializes in children, their practice should be at least 50% children.)
2. What ages of children do you work with? (To ensure they are working with kids in the age range of your children.)
3. What is your past experience in working with children of divorce? (Do they have experience in this focus area?)
4. What is your overall philosophy regarding working with children and families of divorce? Do you have a proactive approach? (To understand why they do this work and what about it is important to them.)
5. Have you attended any specialized training to focus on children and divorce? (To see if this area is a focus of further training for them.)
6. How do you work with children, what is your model? (To help you to understand if they just sit and talk, if they do activities, or how they ensure your child is getting what they need in the therapy.)
7. How many years have you been practicing and what is your personal background with divorce? (This will tell you how long they have been in this field and what personal experience they have with divorce.)
8. If you take insurance, do you have to diagnose my child for insurance purposes? (This can lead to your child being diagnosed with disorders so that the therapist can be paid. This is something that concerns me ethically as a therapist right now in our current mental health system. I believe this is at least important for parents to be aware of.)

Misunderstood Need #3: Telling Your Children About The Divorce: They Need To Know What Is Happening From Both Parents

The best route to take in telling your children you and their other parent are divorcing/separating is to be honest without sharing intimate details and/or subjective emotional opinion about what happened. Telling children can be one of the most difficult conversations parents will have with their children. Following the guidelines below will you help have this conversation with your child in the best manner possible for you and your child. There is also a sample outline of the conversation below.

Items To Consider <u>Before</u> Telling Your Child You Are Divorcing

1. Make sure that this is a final decision, that you have done all you are going to do to make your marriage work, and you now know that the only alternative is divorce. This does not always mean both parents want the divorce but it means you are sure there are no other options for your family right now. It is very hard on your children when parents go back and forth, so just be sure about your decision to tell the children.

2. Ask yourself, are you emotionally stable enough to be there for your child in this meeting? This meeting can set the stage for the rest of this divorce process. Your child will need you right now. Your job in this conversation is to focus on the needs of your child and be available for their concerns and questions.

3. It is important in this conversation to not make promises that you cannot keep. This can be a challenge because things change. Be realistic with your words and promises, children remember promises and this can undermine trust later. If you don't know something, just be honest with your child.

4. It can be difficult to explain to your children the reason for your separation or divorce. Parents always want to know what is best to tell their children. I do believe in being honest with your child because not being honest can

undermine their trust later. However, there should be no intimate details shared. Some things may be too much for them to hear at this time and would be better addressed in the future. This is true in cases of infidelity, drug/alcohol usage, etc. Never in this meeting should one person be blamed. This will not be helpful to your child during this difficult conversation. The simple way to say it is, "We no longer make each other happy and we can't meet each other's needs." In most cases, I also believe it is best that both parties take responsibility for the marriage ending. Most therapists agree that both spouses have contributed to the marital break-up.[29] I would suggest trying to look at your part in the relationship's ending and see if it seems right to share this with your children—but again, without sharing intimate details. If you both agree that this has been more one parent's choice than the other's, then you can tell this to the child. You still want to be careful to not blame that person, but if they want to accept responsibility for the choice that is fine.

5. Next decide where and when you will tell your children. Usually in the home is best and it should certainly not be in a public place. You want them to be able to go to their room to comfort themselves or go outside after if they need to. If at all possible don't tell them right near bedtime. Also don't tell them if one parent is planning on going out of town the next day. Be there for your child for at least a week after the initial conversation when possible.

6. If at all possible, tell your children together. Both parents should be there and all of your children should be present. This is best because both parents are there to respond to your children's questions. It also reassures your children when you are both present. They are clear this is a decision both of you have been involved in. You may have to make some age-appropriate choices in the words you use, but if the kids are all together, they will all hear the same message, which is important. You can talk with them individually after the conversation if they have further questions.

7. It is OK to cry. Parents think that they have to be strong but this belief is not necessarily true. If you cry, your child feels it is OK for them to cry, too. Crying is healthy, we are allowing ourselves to feel and express our true feelings when we cry. I do not recommend crying the entire time or crying so much that you can't talk. Some emotion is good, excessive emotion is not during this conversation. If you find yourself in the place of not being able to stop crying when you tell your children, excuse yourself for a few minutes, go to the bathroom, take some deep breaths, tell yourself you can do this and return to your children. They need your strength right now. If you know this will be difficult for you, I encourage you to take time and cry prior to the meeting on your own. This will assist you in processing so that you can be calmer in front of your children. Remember, your children rely on you for safety and security. If they sense you feel unsafe, this will create additional stress for your child.

8. If the discussion gets angry or someone is very upset, take a time out and say that you will get back together in a few minutes. If the other parent happens to blame you, work to remain calm and let your children know that divorce can make people upset.

9. Decide who will start out the conversation with your children. You should take turns if possible, using the outline below as a guide. Only say what is honest for you.

10. Decide what you know for certain and will tell the children. Know this before you go into the meeting with your children (i.e., mom/dad will live in an apartment, you will live <u>at</u> (location) and go to the same school for the rest of this year). Make sure you write these out and agree on these before the meeting with the children.

Sample Conversation Outline

Please don't just read this, take the points that make most sense in your situation and customize them to your situation.

- Dad/mom and I have something very important to discuss with you.

- We want you to know that we love you very much.
- We want you to know that we were happy when we met.
- We loved each other very much.
- We were so happy when you were born, you were such a beautiful gift to us.
- Our partnership/marriage, your birth and parenting brought us happiness.
- You were created from a place of love (make sure your child feels wanted).
- We will both be in your life forever.
- Dad/mom and I have decided that we no longer make each other happy. We don't meet each other's needs and have grown apart.
- We have tried to work this out, we have gone to counseling (whatever is true for your family).
- This is sad for us.
- We have decided that we will get a divorce. Do you know what that means? Explain divorce in whatever terms your child's age warrants. Younger kids need to know that you won't live together anymore and that you won't be married. You will have separate homes. Explain that divorce is only something that happens between adults.
- We want you to know that this is not your fault, it has nothing to do with you. This is because your dad/ mom and I no longer make each other happy and that has absolutely nothing to do with you. You will never have to choose between us.
- We want you to understand that there are different kinds of love. Sometimes when parents love each other, that love just does not grow and has to end. But that is very different than a parent and child's love. When a parent has a child, they are bonded to that child forever. Even if we get upset with you or are angry, we will NEVER leave you. We both love you and that will always be there. You will always have both of us in your life (if this is true for your family). Draw this out visually for them if they are younger. Show you and your child connected forever. You can clasp your hands together as well to show this visually.

Sidebar regarding the above bullets: Another point I want to make here is that I have sometimes heard parents say to kids, "Your dad/mom is divorcing us." Be clear, your co-parent did NOT divorce their children. Statements like this are emotionally damaging for your children to hear. Do not bring your children into the middle of your stuff. They are not being divorced, bottom line.

Conversation With Child (Continued)

- Right now, these are the things we know will impact you (make sure to agree with your co-parent on these ahead of time). Tell them what you know will change and what you know will stay the same.
- We want to involve you in this process as much as we can.
- This will be a family process. We want to involve you in this and hear your thoughts and opinions. And, as parents, we will have to make final decisions (you don't want your children to be ultimately responsible for the final decisions but you want their input).
- We love you so very much. We will both be here, we will both take care of you.
- We will discuss ways that this can work the best for all of us.
- What questions do you have? (If your child asks questions that you do not know the answer to or you may not agree on, tell them mom and dad will discuss it and get back to them with answers).

Sidebar about the above bullets: I recommend you involve your children in the decisions impacting them when and as much as possible. This does not mean your children make the final decisions. You are the adult and are responsible for that. It means you will allow them to have input, consider it, and incorporate it wherever, whenever possible. In Australia, children are involved in the mediation process, which is creating a better overall result for everyone in the family.[32]

If you already know one person is going to move out, make sure you tell your children, "Even though mom/dad is moving out, I (the person moving out) will still be in your life. I will be here with you whenever you need me." You also want to tell them that the parent that is staying will always be with them, too, especially if your situation is that one parent has left and you are not sure if they will be part of your child's life. Children sometimes fear that if one parent has left, the parent they live with will leave as well.

Answer their questions the best that you can. Blaming one person does not help anything. It certainly does not help your child right now in the middle of this scary situation. If it is true that only one person wants the divorce, you can tell your children that. However, this is not the time or place for blame. Your children are dealing with enough right now, they do not need to be brought into your emotional struggles. The truth is, if one person wants the divorce, at some point it must be a joint decision because that will be the healthiest option for everyone involved. If you truly want to stay married to someone that has no desire to be with you, I believe that you must do some reflection on why that is, please see *Chapter 6: Choosing To Heal Yourself*, for more information on this topic.

Conversation With Child (Continued)

- You can always come to us with any fears or concerns you have. If your child already has a therapist you can also encourage them to share any fears or concerns with this person at their next visit.
- Hug your children and look them squarely in the face and tell them how much you love them. Close the discussion by telling your child the following:

  "We love you and we are all going to be OK. Your mom is here for you and your dad is here for you (or whatever may be the case in your family). We are going to work together."

Conversation Continued With Your Child—Into The Next Few Weeks

Remember to keep your child informed as things change and progress. A weekly meeting would be a good idea so that children feel that they know what is happening in the process. This will lessen your child's anxiety. Initially check in with your child every couple of days to make sure they are doing OK and to allow them to express any concerns to you.

Conversation Continued With Your Child—As They Grow

As your child grows, you will want to come back and revisit this conversation about what happened. Especially if your child is younger when the divorce occurs, because if you don't do this, they will make up what happened.[31] What I have learned in my work with kids is that even if they were only a baby when their parents' divorced, when they are older they will make it about them. A 9-year-old boy whose parents divorced when he was a baby, said he thought it was because he was bad. It is important at each developmental stage (see developmental stages in the Appendix) to talk to your child about the end of your marriage and what happened. During these times, you can tell your child what your hopes for their future are, and reassure them of your confidence in their ability to succeed in love and life.

Misunderstood Need #4: The Need For Consistency, Structure, Rules And Discipline

Children thrive on consistency. They need this in their lives to feel safe and secure. When children feel safe and secure, they have the foundation that allows them to appropriately grow and develop.

Children Need Consistency

Parenting plans create a structure of consistency for the new family structures. Parenting plans are usually seen as a way to split parenting time. I would like to suggest that parenting plans also include the logistics of how you will co-parent your child. You will want to take time to develop a thorough plan. Please see the Appendix for a sample parenting plan. I recommend looking at resources on the internet and you can find sample parenting plan links at www. healthychildrenofdivorce.com. Courts also usually have a template for a parenting plan if you look at their website.

If you and your co-parent can agree to it, you should include consistency between the two homes in your agreement. This would include issues such as bedtime, food choices, rules regarding curfews, use of profanity, screen time (TV, computer, games), etc. You may not agree on all of these things but remember that it will be easier for your child if there is a level of consistency between their homes—they will appreciate the continuity they feel in their lives. You may have to compromise with your co-parent for the best interest of your child.

Regarding communication and your child feeling that their parents agree on discipline, I will share the following story. I met a woman once who divorced when her son was eight-years old. She and her son's father had dinner together every Wednesday to discuss any issues with their son. Their son actually attended these dinners. Their son was clear that his parents would communicate on all of his important life issues. This provided a solid environment for their son to grow and develop. Their son is now a happily married and well-adjusted 30-year old. He thanked his parents at his wedding for how civil they had been. He told them he had seen how other friends' divorced parents behaved, and he appreciated how lucky he had been to have two parents who could communicate so well. This arrangement certainly may not be possible in many families, but it is a great example of what parents have been able to do for the sake of their child.

If at all possible, and your child is doing well at their current school, it would be healthy for them to be able to remain at their same school at least for the full school year. This ensures that they can continue their friendships and support system. It also keeps one thing familiar in a sea of changes. It is very important to alert your child's teacher of the change occurring in your family. Teachers see your child every day and they can assist you in identifying any early-warning signs that your child is experiencing stress. It is crucial for your child that both parents work together to assist with homework and projects. Ensure that your child has a school system (backpack, folders, supplies, etc.) that both of you are aware of so you can assist your child with organizing and maintaining school work. Children report this is one of the most stressful aspects of going between two homes, that they lose homework or do not get homework done due to feeling disorganized.

You will also need to agree on actual parenting time with your child. There are many examples of parenting time schedules to be found on the internet. For some excellent information on parenting time schedules go to www. healthychildrenofdivorce.com. The important thing to remember is that if you and your co-parent are still in conflict, you need to limit the amount of contact you have with your co-parent. Arrange transitions (drop-offs and pick-ups) at school or daycare, where you don't have to see your co-parent or choose a neutral site, like a family friend's house, your church, or a public library if you have to see them.

There are many options depending on your child's age. You also want to take into consideration your child's needs as well. I have known children who did not like going back and forth so frequently and asked for a full week at each home. Remember, this plan is to meet the needs of your child, not your needs. If you are having a hard time being away from your child, get your own support. Do not make this your child's issue. I sometimes recommend, if your child is having difficulty being apart for a week, have dinner with your child every Wednesday when it is not your week. If possible, pick your child up from school and drop them off at their other parent's when you are done eating.

Children Need Discipline And Rules

The word discipline actually means "to teach." Discipline in life teaches your child to be a well-adjusted, contributing member of society. Teaching them to have discipline regarding the fact they have to follow rules is giving them skills for their entire life. Discipline is not the same as punishment. If consequences for behavior are needed, I recommend using natural and logical consequences (see Chapter 9 Effective Parenting After Divorce Strategies).

Discipline is actually showing love to your child. It includes structure and rules, setting limits, time outs and natural consequences, talking about thoughts and feelings of

Discipline (from Latin, *disciplinare*) def. **"to teach"**

the child, and teaching your child respect for themselves, others and their things.[33] Discipline also includes having your child involved in chores and contributing around the home (see Appendix for list of chores/responsibilities for different ages). All of these things are crucial for your child's healthy growth and development. I encourage you to see discipline as a positive thing that you can do for your child so they can be successful in life.

Misunderstood Need #5: The Importance Of Friends And Home Environment

Your child will need their friends during this time. They need to be able to have fun with friends. Friends are a crucial aspect of your child's development. If one parent has moved into an area where your child does not know anyone, it is extremely important to: 1) invite friends over to your new home from your child's other neighborhood or school; 2) attend activities in your new area where your child can meet new potential friends—YMCA, community events, etc.; 3) meet your neighbors, get to know them and find out if they have children your child's age. Get to know the families and invite the children over to play.

If you are a dad or mom who may only see your child on the weekends, it may happen that your child sometimes won't want to see you because they have a party they were invited to or they want to go to an activity with their friends. This type of schedule conflict will usually increase as your child gets older but it will also happen when they are younger. My advice is to talk about this with your child right away. Let them know that you support them spending time with their friends and that they should let you know when they have an activity that might interfere with the normal visitation schedule. Hopefully, you will be able to create a win-win situation for your child where they can communicate with you about their needs and you can work out the best possible (compromise) solution with them. This may mean you see your child a bit less, but I can assure you that your child needs this time with their friends—it's part of being a kid. Your child should not be punished for their parent's divorce. Find creative ways to be part of this event. You could drop them off and pick them up, participate if it is a school or extracurricular event, get to know other parents, etc. I know this can feel unfair. It also feels unfair to your child to not be able to see their friends. Another idea is to work with your child's other parent to see if there is another day that you could see your child or if you could maybe take your child to dinner that week. I ask those parents that have the child for the majority of the time to be sensitive and work with your child's other parent to ensure your child gets to be with their friends and is also able to see their other parent. I have utmost faith you can work together for the greatest good of your child.

The home environment is very important. It is essential that your child not have to drag everything back and forth between homes. Over time, it is my recommendation that you build up two sets of everything your child needs at each parent's home. While this can be expensive initially, if you can, include it into the budget around the divorce. This should be an expense born by both parents when possible as part of the divorce settlement. The impact of your divorce should be as minimal as possible on your child. They should not hear comments like, "Your dad did not send your clothes." Or, "It is so expensive having to buy all of these things." This is *not* your child's issue. Your child also needs to have their own space at each home. Even if this looks like a set of drawers and some space that is just theirs, your child needs this.

Children have reported that they don't feel they have a true home because they feel like they are just visitors at each home. This can be especially true if parents remarry and have more children with their new partner. Do not let this happen to your child. Be sure that they know your home is their home when they are with you. Do whatever it takes to ensure this.

The next idea may invoke some stressful feelings in some parents. It is important, if they want it, for your child to have pictures of their other parent at your home. They can simply have a photo book that they can look at when they want to. They will miss this other parent and it is healthy for them to have this reminder. It would also be healthy for you to encourage your child to let you know when they miss their other parent. You can help them process their feelings of sadness. It will help your child to be able to talk about their feelings.

Misunderstood Need #6: Not Understanding The Grief Process Of Your Child And Your Family

It was really amazing when I realized through my early research that divorce is like a death. It is the death of a dream and the death of a family the way you knew it. You will grieve, your children will grieve and your friends and family will grieve. When I received an email from my friend that she and her husband were divorcing, I cried. I was sad for this ending even though it truly had nothing to do with me. It is important to be aware of the grief process your family will go through so you know what is happening to you and others. These feelings may manifest in strange ways.

> **"Facing your most horrible weakness is something you can do to strengthen your children."**
> —Mary Ellen Hannibal

JoAnn's Story

A friend of mine, JoAnn is going through a difficult divorce. She recently told me that her mother let her know she was going to start taking Prozac. My friend asked her mother why. Her mother's response was that she feels so sad and depressed due to loosing someone she thought of as a son.

Elisabeth Kubler-Ross and David Kessler described several stages of grief related to death and dying. These stages are usually presented in a linear format; however, the process of going through these stages is anything but linear. You will experience them in various order and may jump around from one to the other. However, in some cases, people move through them exactly as they are described. Just be aware that you may move into acceptance one week only to find yourself "back" in anger the next week. Every family member will usually move through these stages differently. The authors also explained that all the stages were not always experienced by her clients but she stated a person always will experience at least two.

The Five Stages Of Grief

"This can't be happening to me." This is a stage of disbelief/shock.

"This is not fair, this is all their fault." "I am so angry at them." "I am so angry at myself."

"Life goes on, it will be ok." "I will be ok."

"This is so sad." "I am so sad." "Life is so unfair."

"I will do whatever it takes to make this work." "What can I do?" "I will be a good kid/parent if we can make this work."

Based on "The Grief Cycle" in Elizabeth Kubler-Ross and David Kessler's, *On Death and Dying*, 1969

It is important to recognize when you are going through each of these stages. It is important to go through each of the grief stages, they are healing stages. What you need to be aware of is being "stuck" at one stage. My parents were stuck for a long time at the anger stage. If you are angry or depressed, you are still feeling some type of hurt. Your anger may be because you still feel rejected. You feel you are no longer loved and are no longer lovable or worthy of love. Anger and depression can be the response to this.[34] If you are stuck at one stage, it is so challenging for your children to effectively move on. If a parent is stuck at one stage, it can create impairment in your child's development. The reason for this is that the parent is not available to the child to help them grow and face the stresses of life if they are still stuck and wallowing in their pain.[35] If you have any suspicion this could be you, you should seek help immediately. As Mary Ellen Hannibal says, "Facing your most horrible weakness is something you can do to strengthen your children."

If you use your anger to keep your child away from their other parent or to say negative things about the other parent, you are using it destructively. It is healthy to release and let go of your anger, but children should not in any way be part of this release.

A few words on sadness, just as with anger, it is healthy to allow ourselves to be sad. If we feel like crying but hold it back, that feeling gets stuffed inside of us. When we allow ourselves to have the feelings, it releases them and we can feel so much better mentally and physically. Letting it go creates space inside of us. I read Brandon Bays' book, *The Journey.* Bays had some really terrible things occur in her life, so she shut off everything and stayed in her home for a week and cried. She let all the emotion out that she could. Everyone will deal with sadness differently, but releasing emotion allows us to heal and provides space for us to bring other good things into our life. I truly believe, based on my own experience and that of others I have counseled, that the sadness you are feeling now is not just about this person but it is also about other losses and life experiences you have had. If you or your child ever have thoughts of harming yourself, it is important to seek professional help immediately. Ensure your children have the support they need.

It is important to understand that during this time children can sometimes use play and fantasy as ways to heal. Some children during this time resort to fantasies. Withdrawal into fantasy can serve an important role in allowing your child to work through their reactions to the separation and divorce. Play and fantasy can be very good for children. Parents should not discourage this unless it interferes with school and play with other children.[36] Children are amazingly resilient and may find very creative ways to deal with their feelings of loss and sadness.

Misunderstood Need #7: Not Understanding Children's Feelings And Fears

The following is a list of children's feelings that are important for you to know about and understand as a parent.[37]

1. Children fear abandonment and worry about who will take care of them. We have discussed this already but it is crucial to ensure your child knows you will always be there to care for them.
2. Children usually want parents to get back together and have difficulty accepting that parents won't reunite. Children do many things to try to get their parents to stay together or to get back together. It is normal that children would prefer to have their family together. However, in cases of very high conflict, it can be normal for children to feel relieved about their parents' divorce.
3. Children blame themselves for the divorce. Most children are amazingly egocentric. Especially when they are younger, they feel that the world revolves around them. Given this view, it makes sense that they believe that in some way they are responsible for their parents' divorce. Children will usually feel some guilt around the divorce. In my case, I felt guilty that as a child I had wished that my parents would divorce because of the high conflict in their marriage. Even college-age children whose parents divorce feel they are to blame. They sometimes think if they had not left home, their parents would not have divorced. They especially can feel guilt if you are fighting with their other parent over issues related to them. Remember to let your children know, whatever their ages, that your divorce is not their fault.
4. Children may feel frustration if they feel that they are not being heard. It is so important to listen to your child's fears, concerns and needs during this time.
5. Children feel stress about loyalty issues during the divorce. Children want to be able to freely love each of their parents. Do not ask your child to take sides or give your child negative information about the other parent. Bashing your child's other parent increases your child's stress.
6. Children will do anything to please you and help you with your emotional struggles due to their fears about your well-being. If you are not doing well, this feels scary

to your child. You are the one they need for support and safety. If you are emotionally upset, they will want you to get better, they love you and want you to be happy. It is not your child's job to take care of you; make sure *you* are taking care of yourself.

Misunderstood Need #8: Not Understanding The Developmental Stage Of Your Child And Its Importance

The developmental stage your child is in when you divorce effects how they will react to the divorce. If the divorce causes your child extreme stress, your child's development can be delayed or stalled at this point. Divorce can impact the development process of your child. Development is so crucial because it is how your child builds their sense of self. It is important to understand your child's developmental stage so you can address any issues they may experience and needs they may have at this time related to the divorce/separation.[38] If you address your child's fears as stated in the previous section, your child will have an easier time of progressing through their appropriate developmental stages. See Appendix for ages and stages of development.

Your child may regress to a previous development stage or exhibit childish behaviors during this time. Regressive behavior is common and normal during an event like divorce. It is OK to indulge your child initially, but any indulgence should not last longer than four to six weeks and then be gradually reduced, otherwise it will become a pattern.[39] Regressive behaviors usually happen with younger children and can include: thumb sucking, baby talk, whining, being more demanding, wanting the bottle again, wetting/soiling their clothes, temper tantrums and/or clinging. One common behavior in divorce situations is the child sleeping in the parent's bed or the parent sleeping or falling asleep with the child. Parents must be sure that this behavior is not meeting their own need to feel secure and safe. At some point, having your child sleep with you is not healthy for you or your child, because having a parent sleep with a child does not allow your child to develop into an independent, confident person.

My friend either slept with her nine-year-old daughter so her daughter could get to sleep, or allowed her daughter in her bed on many occasions. So what happened when her daughter went to sleep-over camp? Her daughter had trouble going to sleep each night. It is crucial to make sure that you are not overcompensating for your children during this time as it will impact their ability to develop socially. Sleepovers at friend's or family members' homes can be challenging for these children if they are used to going to sleep with their parent. Reading to your child at bedtime is great one-on-one time, but let them know that they need to go to sleep by themselves and that you have confidence that they can do it. If your child expresses anxiety, tell them they will be fine, that you are not far away, and that it is now time for them to go to sleep on their own. I have worked with parents who have been successful in using a system that rewards the child for staying in their own bed for a consecutive number of nights.

Whether it is sleeping with you or allowing some other regressive behavior to continue, you also could be overindulging your child's regressive behavior out of your own guilt over their pain or loss over your divorce. This is not helpful for your child. Again, it is OK to allow the regressive behaviors initially but don't allow them to become a habit.[40] You will empower your child if you have confidence in them and in their ability to move forward.

Be aware that long term after the divorce, as your child progresses through later developmental stages, the issue of the divorce may resurface. They also may experience blocks or issues/concerns in relationships as a result of the divorce. These are areas that are good for you to be aware of so you can communicate about them with your child. As your child moves into the dating stage it may be helpful to explore any concerns that they may have about themselves and their relationships as they relate to the divorce.

Misunderstood Need #9: Thinking This Divorce Will Not Impact Your Adult Child

My parents officially divorced when I was twenty-one. For me, honestly, my parents' divorce was an end to a really long road of 21 years of fighting, anger and conflict. My parents first filed for divorce when I was 11 but did not go through with it. Ten-years later, when they did divorce, I had a huge grief reaction. I didn't understand my emotional reaction at the time. I remember my mom saying to me in an accusing and surprised tone, "You are taking this worse than your sisters." My sisters were then nine and eleven and had not lived through all the conflict that I had, though they had seen their share. Even at 21, my initial reaction was grief.

In a recent questionnaire that I gave to some parents, I asked what was the most significant and sad event of your life. One parent answered, "My parents divorcing when I was an adult." No matter what age your child is when you divorce, they will have a reaction.

I also believe that if your child is old enough to be in a dating relationship when your divorce happens, that they may have greater struggles in that relationship. My boyfriend at the time and I endured two divorces (his parents' and my parents') during our relationship. I think it would be quite surprising if we would have stayed together given the amount of stress and marriage failure that emerged during our relationship. I also have seen other kids of divorce who were dating during their parents' divorce, have their relationships end. I have no statistical data on this, but I believe divorce can negatively impact the child's other relationships. It is something that we do not think about as children of divorce. It is something to be aware of if your child is dating when you go through the divorce, no matter what their age. My recommendation is to have a conversation with them that the divorce could bring up fears for them about the success of their relationship and that they should be aware of this. I do wish I'd had the opportunity to look at this at the time. It may be helpful for your adult child to seek counseling depending on their situation.

Just remember, that whatever age your children are, your divorce will impact them in one way or another. The best way to approach this is to talk to your children and make them aware that they may have a reaction to the divorce. No matter what your child's age, even adult children, when you divorce, you will still want to tell them:

- You loved their other parent at one time.
- You were happy when they were born.
- You tried to make the marriage work.
- They were not the cause of your fighting.
- You and your co-parent no longer make each other happy.
- You will be here for them should they need anything.
- You love them very much.
- You know this could bring up old feelings. It could cause them to have a reaction, and you are there for them if they want to talk.
- You encourage them to attend counseling to process the divorce if that feels right to them.
- If they are old enough to be in dating relationship, that the divorce could bring up some fears in that relationship, too.

Misunderstood Need #10: Not Understanding Your Child's Need For Extended Family

There are two areas to consider regarding your child and their extended family. The first area is that children of divorce sometimes see their extended family less frequently than prior to the divorce. In some cases they may even lose total contact. Prior to divorce, extended family members may have provided your child regular support and love. After divorce, it is sometimes the case that children do not see their extended family members as much due to schedules, moving and ongoing conflict between adults over the divorce, etc. For example, an annual family gathering of your child's other parent may fall on your weekend. It would be in the best interest of your child to allow them to attend that party because they will be able to feel supported and loved by their extended family. You do not want to take this opportunity away from your child. Even if the circumstances are that your co-parent has checked out but his or her family wants to be involved with your child, it is important to honor this family relationship for your child. It can be very healthy for your child to maintain this family connection, which can help them feel valued and loved.

The second area to understand is that sometimes children want more time with their extended family. Sometimes children may not have had a lot of prior contact with extended family prior to the divorce/separation. In some cases, after a divorce, children may want to see cousins or grandparents they have not spent much time with. Their other parent may have a problem with this, especially if the child did not see this side of the family very much prior to the divorce. It is common for children to want to be connected with their family. Family can be very important to children and positively impact their growth and development. Judith Wallerstein found in her studies that children with a close relationship with grandparents reported an easier childhood.[41] If your child reaches an age and has a desire to have more contact with your ex-spouse's family and has not had a lot of contact with them in the past, do not be surprised. Allow your child this connection, it is supportive for them to know and love their family.

Misunderstood Need #11: Not Understanding Your Child's Need To Have Some Control And To Have Easy Transitions Between Homes

In this section, the goal is to assist you in understanding the lack of control that children of divorce feel. Children of divorce do not have control regarding whether or not their parents choose to stay married. They sometimes are told many things that will happen to them or that will change in their lives without their being included in decisions. I encourage you to involve your children as much as possible in decisions impacting them, as I suggested earlier in this chapter. However, they should never be the final decision maker and you should make this clear to them. That is your role as the parent. I also encourage you to allow your child to make as many decisions as possible regarding other things that are smaller, less impactful choices. Be creative here. If you move into a new place, for example, allow them to paint their bedroom whatever color they want. If you have them on the weekend, give them choices of things to do. For children of divorce, it is important to feel that children have some choice in a world that may feel *choiceless* at times. During this process you want to empower your children as much as possible. Giving children choices is very empowering. You also want them to know that you respect and trust their choices.

> **"It is important to feel that children have some choice in a world that may feel choiceless at times."**

Transitions

It is important to realize that transitions represent change to a child. We know how humans respond to change, they usually resist it in some way. Your child may have difficulty transitioning from one parent to the other. They may cry and want to stay with you. This does not necessarily mean that they fear their other parent. It usually means they fear change, which scares them. Going back and forth between parents can be a very challenging thing for your child to get used to.

Your Children Need Transition Time

Some children have more trouble with this than others. A child I was working with was acting out after visiting her father for the summer. Her mother was sure something bad had happened while she was with her father. When I asked the girl why she was acting out she said, "I think it is because I miss my dad." You must have empathy and patience with your children during transitions. Some children may return home and need to sleep for a few hours, others may need to have one-on-one time with you. One parent I worked with said the time of transition was very crucial for her child as well. If her child came home near bedtime, her child had a difficult time settling down. The solution was to have the child home earlier because they had school the next day.

Many parents report when children come back earlier in the day, they just need to sleep. It is very important to understand that each child will react differently to the transition between homes. Recognize that going between homes and having different schedules and rules can be challenging for your child. A very good strategy is to have a calming ritual when your child returns such as a hot bath, reading a book or just some quiet downtime. It is important to allow your child this time to adjust.

It is your job as a parent to be aware that these transitional behaviors may occur and to help your child make transitions more effectively. Another method of assisting your younger child in transitions is to have an age-appropriate transition object, this may be a favorite toy, blanket, or stuffed animal that is always with the child. Your goal is to make this transition as easy as possible for your child so that they feel safe and secure.

Possible Common Transition Reactions

- Clingy-ness
- Tiredness
- Irritability
- Need to be alone
- Need to be close to you
- Temper tantrums
- Oppositional behavior—testing limits again
- Regressive behaviors

Assisting Your Younger Child With Transitions

- Prepare them ahead of time, in the morning, by letting them know this is their day to be with their other parent.
- About an hour before it is time to go, ask them to make sure they have everything ready that they want to take with them.
- Remind them again about 15 minutes before it is time to transition. If your child has difficulty with transitions, several reminders can be helpful so that when the time comes they are mentally very prepared. If they are resisting, tell them something positive like, "I remember last time you had fun at the park, I bet mom has something fun planned for this week."

- Make sure you are acting positively about this transition. It is important for your child to know you are OK with them going to see their other parent. This applies to your words, your tone and your body language.
- Remind them when you will see them again, that you love them and to have a good time with their other parent.

Misunderstood Need #12: Not Understanding The Underlying Reasons For Your Child's Misbehavior

It is important to remember that when your child is acting out, that emotionally they are not doing well. They have some big feelings going on inside and they are acting out because they don't feel good inside. When your child acts out, it is crucial to look deeper to see why they may be acting out at this time and what could be going on for them emotionally that is causing them to act out.

"When your child acts out, they are usually acting out in response to something going on in their environment."

Children do not want to misbehave. When your child acts out, they are usually acting out in response to something going on in their environment. It is important to always remember this and try to understand why your child may be exhibiting the inappropriate behavior.

It is also important to remember that children want your attention. They will do what it takes to get it, even if that means exhibiting negative behavior. Children will escalate their behavior until they feel heard by you.[42] I always notice when I go to the homes of my friends' who have small children, that the child will begin acting out as soon as their parents' attention is on me. They really want to know their parent is aware they are there and that the parent is focusing on them. This attention-getting phenomenon reminds me of what I have seen when I have volunteered at an orphanage. Children in orphanages who fall and bump their heads just get back up without crying. They have learned that no one will come to help them, so they do not cry because it does not create any response. Be glad your children are crying for your attention. Listen to them and look deeper to understand what their behavior is trying to tell you.

Misunderstood Need #13: Not Understanding Your Child's Parenting-Time Needs Change As They Grow

The other situation that may occur is when your child becomes a teenager, they may have a desire to live with or spend more time with their same-sex parent if they have not previously. Children want to "know" their other parent and identify more closely with how their same-sex parent approaches the world. Do not take this personally, it is a developmental need.

If you have a daughter, around the time she is 12-years old, she may have a different reaction to spending time alone with dad. This behavior is recognized as a normal stage of development for some girls as they move into womanhood.[43] This reaction will usually vary depending upon how much time the father and daughter previously spent together. If she has been with him for the majority of her childhood, this will probably be a lot less prevalent. If it happens that your daughter now has some reservations about spending time alone with dad, here are some suggestions. First, allow her to bring friends to the visits on occasion; second, ask her what activities she would like to do; and third, talk to her about how she may be feeling as she matures.

In summary, kids are amazing and they have so many needs. As a parent, you are doing the best job you can if you take time to understand and address your child's needs. In Chapter 9 we will discuss more ways you can effectively meet your child's needs.

Questions For Reflection:

What needs of my child do I need to be more aware of?

_____

_____

_____

_____

_____

What can I do to be more supportive of my child and their needs?

_____

_____

_____

_____

_____

_____

_____

_____

_____

_____

_____

_____

_____

_____

_____

_____

~~6~~

Fatal Mistake #5: Choosing Not To Heal Your Pain And Not To Take Responsibility For Your Actions

Sometimes when relationships end, it can be difficult to move forward with our lives. We may choose to stay stuck in the pain versus push through it to move forward with our lives. Ask yourself the following questions:

1. Do I still feel angry with my child's other parent?
2. Do I still feel very sad, like I can't move on because I am still upset?
3. Do I still blame my child's other parent for my pain and hurt?

If you answered Yes to any of the above, you may be choosing, consciously or unconsciously, to stay stuck. You do have to move through the stages of grief, and there is no fixed time limit for that to occur, however, wherever you are in the grieving process, this chapter will help you move forward. This

> **"A person can only love someone to the extent that they love themselves."**
> —Michael Oddenino

place of being stopped can sometimes feel safer and easier than taking the steps to move forward. It may be unclear to you what steps you need to take. The truth is that if you are choosing to stay stuck, you are choosing to not move on from this relationship. You could also feel that you are punishing your child's other parent. However, you are truly punishing yourself and your child by not moving forward. While it may be true that your co-parent hurt you or wronged you in some way, the truth is that you were 50% of that relationship. You now have to make a choice. You can choose to move on to create a healthy environment for you and your child or you can stay stuck in a place of anger and pain over a relationship that no longer exists. You can be the victim, but know that victims are not healthy parents.

I am not minimizing how challenging this can seem, I just want you to understand that you have a choice. This chapter will assist you in moving forward. It will assist you, if you allow it, in letting go. It will allow you to begin to live your life fully again, or maybe for the first time. The very good news is that I completely believe that this experience you have endured can assist you in creating your best life. The catch is that you must view this experience as an opportunity for growth and healing.

> **"People spend a lifetime searching for happiness; looking for peace. They chase idle dreams, addictions, religions, even other people, hoping to fill the emptiness that plagues them. The irony is, the only place they ever needed to search, was within."**
> —Ramona L. Anderson

Am I telling you this process will be easy? No. Am I telling you it is possible to move forward successfully? Yes. I ask you to do this for yourself and for your child. You both deserve it. I know how amazing you are because you are reading this book. You are thinking about your child and you want to be the best parent for your child. You deserve the most amazing life possible. If you use this experience as an opportunity to heal, you will be able to better love yourself and love your child. You will also be able to be a better partner should you decide to pursue that in the future. So, I ask you to go through all of the following exercises and just be open to what may show up for you. One question that you answer in this next section could be a key to unlocking something very important. *You* are important.

Choosing To Heal Ourselves

One thing I have learned as a single person trying to understand relationships is that in order to be the best partner and parent possible, I must choose to heal my own wounds and hurts. Know that you are responsible for your own happiness, that your happiness depends solely on you. You alone have the power to create your happiness.[44] As humans, I believe it is completely common for us to look to someone else to help us heal and feel loved. We usually play this out in the form of our romantic relationships. The deeper the pain we felt as children, the deeper our wounds are to heal through relationships. I have done extensive research, self-reflection and writing on self-love. The most important relationship of all is our relationship with our self. No one else can ever make us feel happy on a deep level, we must do that for ourselves. As Michael Oddenino says: "A person can only love someone to the extent that they love themselves."[45]

Something has become fully clear to me through my own journey working to understand relationships and our role in the success or failure of relationships. We must be aware and reflect on ourselves and our reactions during the relationship and at the end of any relationship. If we do this, we will learn and grow and be able to create better future relationships. Being able to create and sustain healthy relationships is important for us. It also provides a healthy model for our children so they have a better chance of creating good relationships in their lives.

If at this time, you are experiencing intense grief and loss or are the one that feels very abandoned, I recommend Susan Anderson's book, *The Journey from Abandonment to Healing: Turning the End of a Relationship Into a New Life*. This book discusses the stages of abandonment and helps you to understand the actual mental and physical feelings/symptoms you are having. It also provides healing exercises that can assist you in moving forward.

Most people know Dr. Phil McGraw. In his book, *Love Smart*, he gives the following exercise and advice. Dr. Phil tells us we can call ourselves victims but to really change things in your life, you must be truthful with yourself. He says, "This is no time to blame your ex, bad timing or general incompatibility. The buck stops here, with you. You only have control over yourself." He offers the following questions to ask yourself about your relationship that has ended (due to the length of these questions, you may want to use a notebook if you need more space for your answers).

1. What were your problems and frustrations with the relationship?

   _____

   _____

2. What were the problems your partner had with you? Be honest with yourself.

   _____

   _____

3. What are ten key statements about the pain you still feel and the open wounds you still have? Write them down. Honesty is essential.

   _____

   _____

4. For each of the statements you just wrote down, ask yourself: What was my role in this?

   _____

   _____

5. What choices did you make that led to the results you got in your last relationship?

   _____

   _____

6. You teach people how to treat you. Did you teach or allow your partner to treat you badly?

   _____

   _____

7. What do you have to change to get over your last relationship? How do you need to heal?

   _____

   _____

8. What part of your last relationship do you want to leave in the past forever? Only when you acknowledge it can you take the steps to prevent repetition.

_____

_____

9. You need emotional closure. To get that, you need to figure out what is your "minimal effective response"—the least thing you can do to get the closure. It may be yelling and screaming, writing your thoughts down or actually talking to your ex. If you need to take steps to feel that you have stood up for yourself, do it.[46]

_____

_____

Every Relationship Is Some Type Of Mirror

My best example of this is when I was engaged, I told my fiancé, "I just want you to love me; you are not loving me." After the end of this relationship, as I went through my own journey of self-understanding, I realized something very important—I did not love me. I was telling him I wanted him to love me but in effect, I was not loving myself. I also realized I was not good at receiving his love when he did give it to me. Wow, this was a big revelation for me when I realized this truth a year after the end of our relationship. I now had to be accountable for what happened. I had to stop blaming him for the demise of our relationship. At this point, I also realized I was the common denominator in a few unsuccessful relationships and I had to look at what my role was in them.

I realized I had no idea how to love myself. This had not been taught to me. I was the one needing to love me. Were some of his actions not loving? Yes for sure, but truly he was not the only one responsible for the relationship not working. I had chosen him. Something about him had been very attractive to me. He was mirroring to me what I needed so much from myself. If you want to heal your own issues, think back to what angered or angers you most about your child's other parent. This will show you a key to something inside of you. It will be a piece of your puzzle to assist you in knowing true happiness in this lifetime. This may be something you are missing or frustrated about in yourself. This person you chose is truly a gift, I know it does NOT seem like that right now, but they are a teacher for you. This is why you attracted them. In another relationship I said, "He just can't commit to me." A very honest friend said to me, "Are you committed to yourself?" As I looked into this, I realized this guy was not the best guy for me and I was selling out on me. I was not being committed to me by staying in a relationship that was not healthy for me. His not wanting to commit to me was mirroring a lack of commitment I had for myself and loving myself.

Exercise 22.

1. Pick an issue that frustrates you with your ex-partner.

   _____

   _____

   _____

2. Think about what this issue could be reflecting to you in your life. Usually what frustrates us does so because it is mirroring something for us to learn.

   _____

   _____

3. Where in your life is this some type of mirror for you? Ask a friend to help you if this is challenging for you. This person needs to be a true friend (I define a true friend as someone who will kick my butt and love me in the same conversation). You could also engage a therapist to help you through this process.

   _____

   _____

It will be amazing to see what may show up if you truthfully look at this. Honestly, what do you have to lose? Looking at this may provide the perfect distraction for you right now. It is time to move forward and stop blaming others. If you truly want to be happy, look inside and begin to

> **"Help thyself, and God will help thee."**
> — Jean de La Fontaine

take responsibility for your life. The truth is that you are the common denominator in your unsuccessful relationships. You have created everything that is in your life right now. Choose to start taking responsibility for your life. This does not mean beating yourself up mentally. This does not mean blaming yourself. It simply means taking responsibility so you can move forward in life. I believe we make choices, if those choices do not work out, we have the opportunity to learn from them and make different, better choices the next time. If we have chosen to learn from past choices, we are now empowered to make better future choices.

We Choose Partners To Assist Us In Healing Our Own Issues

We choose others (usually unconsciously) to assist us in working through our own life issues, pain or trauma. This usually stems from some issue or situation in our childhood. A perfect example is my friend, whose father is an alcoholic, and she married an alcoholic. Honestly, we would never believe that we would purposely marry an alcoholic, but I see it happen again and again. I truly believe that it is our need to heal the past pain that draws us to these specific individuals. We hope on a subconscious level these individuals will assist us in our healing. So in the case of my friend, possibly some part of her believes if she stops her husband from drinking, she will be able to do what she was never able to do for her dad. It also may be that she hopes her partner will stop drinking for her and show her he loves her, as her father never could. In the process, she may be able to heal her own wounds. On some level, we believe that if we can change this person to really love us differently, we will have resolved our old pain. In the process of either standing up to this person (and standing for ourselves) or helping them heal, we receive our own healing. I want to caution you that helping someone heal so they can love you can be a precarious position. If the person truly heals, this may work well for them and may help you heal, too. However, if this person can't or chooses not to heal, this could be a very unhealthy situation for you. If you are at the point of divorcing, you probably have moved beyond hoping you will be able to help this other person. No matter what has happened in your relationship, hopefully you can see some healing has occurred. Looking at it from this perspective can help you see there were positives in this relationship. I believe children are also involved in the healing process. In some cases I have seen children be the catalysts and the lynchpins for their parent's healing.

The interesting part of this is that we don't usually realize on a conscious level what we are doing. However this happens, we know on some level that this person will help us heal and that is our attraction to them. This healing can be amazingly painful. But if we choose to look at this pain and seek help to consciously understand it and heal it, we can achieve amazing growth. Gabor Mate, M.D. in his book explains it this way: "Our choice of relationship partners is patterned on our interactions with our parental caregivers. This is so even if it may appear superficially that the differences far outweigh any possible resemblance." Many authors agree with me on this aspect of our relationships being tied in closely to our caregivers. For further reading on this topic see Harville Hendrix *Getting the Love that You Want* and John Welwood, *Perfect Love, Imperfect Relationships: Healing the Wound of the Heart.*

When I chose my ex-fiancé, he was emotionally distant. I did not consciously think about that at the time, but it was familiar to me. My father had been very emotionally disconnected from me as I grew up. During my relationship with my fiancé, I always longed for more. I always wanted him to be closer and love me more. This was the same story I had about my own father when I looked at it. I tried so hard to change my fiancé. He never did change and we separated. But three years later he called and apologized to me for not being more available. This conversation healed a lot of old hurt for me because he symbolized my parents who were not available to me in their own ways. When he was able to recognize that this behavior was not OK, it healed some of the old wounds from my parents. I had chosen him to be the adult romantic representation of my parents.

exercise 23

To look at this for yourself, answer the following questions. Take some time with this. It is so crucial and important to truly begin to understand this phenomenon. It can be your key to letting go of the anger and pain you have for your ex-partner. It can be a huge first step to beginning to heal and to letting go. This ability to heal and move forward will benefit you and your child.

1. What did you want from your parent(s) that they were not able to give you (time, love, acceptance, etc.)? How do you feel that you were hurt by your parents (if you feel you were)?

> **"It is not easy to find happiness in ourselves, and it is not possible to find it elsewhere."**
> —Agnes Repplier,
> *The Treasure Chest*

2. What did you always want from your partner that they were never able to give you?
3. What do you see that could be similar to these to unmet wants (from your parent and partner) in your life?
4. What old hurts do you see in yourself that you may have been trying to heal by choosing this person?
5. How is your ex-partner similar to your parents or parent?
6. Why might you have chosen them?
7. If your ex did something really terrible to you, how could this person or pain be a representation of other pain you have suffered in your life?
8. Have you seen this pattern played out (or a similar pattern) before in other relationships?
9. What do you think you need to do to heal this hurt in yourself? What is it that you need to give yourself instead of seeking it from others?
10. Is there something in your life that has now changed for the better due to this relationship? What did you learn?
11. What was the gift that this person gave to you (besides your children)?

   I find this phenomenon of attracting others into our life who assist us in our healing to be truly amazing. And I know it may not feel like that to you right now, but this person can assist you in your healing and growth if you are open and conscious of this possibility. This is a heart-driven phenomenon. I don't believe our mind has any role in this. This can be a challenge to understand. We certainly don't think "Gee, let's marry an alcoholic to resolve our issues with our alcoholic dad." Our egos would NEVER stand for that! I believe we will continue to attract others into our lives to help us with our healing. Honestly, some days this journey of healing is so frustrating, yet we must continue. In other ways it is wonderful because we can truly see the silver lining in our challenging relationships. I can tell you that this journey has progressed for me since I first wrote this and it is worth all the pain you are going through right now. From the time I decided I wanted to fully love me, it took 2.5 years of pain but finally I am feeling so happy solo. It is possible, I am here to prove it. All of our journeys are different. You will have your own. If you choose it, it will work in your favor. Just continue to look inside and you will find the answers to assist you. I truly believe we are all here to grow and love ourselves. Whatever divine power you believe in is ready to help you heal if you ask them and are open to receiving help.

Codependent Co-Parents

Another phenomenon I see occurring in relationships that end in divorce or separation is codependency. Codependent behaviors can prevent you from moving forward from this relationship in a healthy way. This is detrimental to you and your child.

If you have children, this codependency can continue for a very long time if you do not set healthy boundaries for the co-parenting relationship. Setting healthy boundaries and knowing what healthy boundaries look like can be extremely challenging since you possibly have spent

"Codependent behaviors can prevent you from moving forward from this relationship in a healthy way."

many years in this codependent state. It can be very hard for you to see the unhealthy behaviors that codependency fosters. Codependency has been associated with drug and alcohol abuse and if you had this in your family or in your families of origin, you probably have some codependency occurring. However, there does not have to be drug or alcohol abuse in your family to have unhealthy codependent behaviors in your family. Usually one of the first warning signs for parents that they are in a codependent relationship is when they begin dating again and the other co-parent is not able to stay out of their dating life or the new relationship. They may not have been able to see these issues on their own but the new partner is very aware of this unhealthy behavior. The other parent may call unnecessarily, may still need "help" with many things and may truly not be able to let go. It also may be that things have continued "status quo" due to an inability to set good boundaries. This continues until a new person enters the life of one of the parties.

   Below are some characteristics of codependent people and a questionnaire to assist you in identifying signs of codependency. Just to note, codependency can take the form of the person controlling or the person being controlled. It takes both of these aspects to create a codependent relationship.

Characteristics Of Codependent People[47]

- An exaggerated sense of responsibility for the actions of others
- A tendency to confuse love and pity, with the tendency to "love" people they can pity and rescue
- A tendency to do more than their share, all of the time
- A tendency to become hurt when people don't recognize their efforts
  - An unhealthy dependence on relationships. The codependent will do anything to hold on to a relationship; to avoid the feeling of abandonment
- An extreme need for approval and recognition
- A sense of guilt when asserting themselves
- A compelling need to control others

- Lack of trust in self and/or others
- Fear of being abandoned or alone
- Difficulty identifying feelings
- Rigidity/difficulty adjusting to change
- Problems with intimacy/boundaries
- Chronic anger
- Lying/dishonesty
- Poor communications
- Difficulty making decisions

 Questionnaire To Identify Signs Of Codependency[48] This condition appears to run in different degrees, whereby the intensity of symptoms are on a spectrum of severity, as opposed to an all or nothing scale. Please note that only a qualified professional can make a diagnosis of codependency; not everyone experiencing these symptoms suffers from codependency.

1. Do you keep quiet to avoid arguments?
2. Are you always worried about others' opinions of you?
3. Have you ever lived with someone with an alcohol or drug problem?
4. Have you ever lived with someone who hits or belittles you?
5. Are the opinions of others more important than your own?
6. Do you have difficulty adjusting to changes at work or home?
7. Do you feel rejected when significant others spend time with friends?
8. Do you doubt your ability to be who you want to be?
9. Are you uncomfortable expressing your true feelings to others?
10. Have you ever felt inadequate?
11. Do you feel like a "bad person" when you make a mistake?
12. Do you have difficulty taking compliments or gifts?
13. Do you feel humiliation when your child or spouse makes a mistake?

14. Do you think people in your life would go downhill without your constant efforts?
15. Do you frequently wish someone could help you get things done?
16. Do you have difficulty talking to people in authority, such as the police or your boss?
17. Are you confused about who you are or where you are going with your life?
18. Do you have trouble saying "no" when asked for help?
19. Do you have trouble asking for help?
20. Do you have so many things going at once that you can't do justice to any of them?

Melody Beattie, a well-known authority on codependency, asks the following questions in her book, *Codependent No More*, to help you see if you may be codependent:

❏ Do you feel responsible for other people—their feelings, thoughts, actions, choices, wants, needs, well-being and destiny?

❏ Do you feel compelled to help people solve their problems or by trying to take care of their feelings?

❏ Do you find it easier to feel and express anger about injustices done to others than about injustices done to you?

❏ Do you feel safest and most comfortable when you are giving to others?

❏ Do you feel insecure and guilty when someone gives to you?

❏ Do you feel empty, bored and worthless if you don't have someone else to take care of, a problem to solve, or a crisis to deal with?

❏ Are you often unable to stop talking, thinking and worrying about other people and their problems?

❏ Do you lose interest in your own life when you are in love?

❏ Do you stay in relationships that don't work and tolerate abuse in order to keep people loving you?

❏ Do you leave bad relationships only to form new ones that don't work, either?

If you have reason to believe this could be your situation, I strongly recommend that you work with a professional to assist you in setting healthy boundaries and creating new healthy behaviors. You can also use many of the strategies at the end of this chapter to assist you in strengthening yourself to be less codependent. As a codependent co-parent, you will not be modeling healthy behaviors for your child. Codependent relationships have dysfunctional behaviors that will not be good for your children to witness or to model in their own relationships.

> **"So I tell you to ask, and you will receive. Search, and you will find. Knock, and the door will be opened for you."**
> —Luke 11:9

We Are 50% Responsible In Relationships: The Road to Freedom

A relationship is something that is 50% our responsibility. As a child, my parents always tried to blame the other person. They always tried to make the other parent the bad guy and as a child, this was really confusing to me. After years of trying to figure out which of them was truly at blame, I finally realized "it was 50/50." That gave them both equal responsibility for all the chaos. This realization as a young adult was probably one of my most important. It gave me a lot of freedom. Now I did not have to waste anymore energy trying to figure out who was right/wrong or good/bad. What the heck was the point anyway? What good does it truly do anyone? I believe that subscribing to the 50/50 philosophy in relationships provides freedom. If you believe this, no one gets to be a victim. I truly believe there are no long-term victims.

We are only victims of our choice not to be responsible for our lives. Even in the case of infidelity, there were still two people in the relationship. There may have even been some warning signs. In my aunt's case, she had asked her husband numerous times to attend counseling and he would not. She then had an affair. Was the end of the relationship both of their faults? I believe it was. They both played a role in the demise of the relationship. Jones-Soderman and Quattrocchi state that an affair is a symptom, not a cause and encourage parents not to blame the divorce on the affair.[49] I want to be clear, I am not saying that affairs are OK, but usually, if you look deeply, both parties had some role in not nurturing the relationship in healthy ways.

Foster Cline, at a recent presentation, discussed that some marriages survive affairs.[50] I believe that many conditions have to be right for this to happen but that it would take both parties being responsible for choosing this relationship and choosing to heal together to move beyond an affair. The bottom line on all of this is that you chose the other person you were in a relationship with for some reason. It is time now to choose to be responsible for your half of the successes and failures. It does not mean you are a failure, just that the relationship between the two of you was not successful on some level. Relationships take work on the part of both people. Taking responsibility is a road to freedom. It frees us from victimhood, which can keep us seriously stuck. If you are stuck, look at why you may be choosing to stay stuck. If you are still not co-parenting well after years of separation and/or divorce, please take a look at yourself and ask why are you doing this. Living in the past is not the way to live. The path to freedom is to move into the future. Ask yourself the following questions:

Exercise 25: Ask yourself the following questions:

1. What is my pay-off for continuing to blame my ex-partner and staying stuck in this relationship's pain/anger? Whenever we are staying stuck somewhere,

> "When you are stuck in your anger and sadness, you are not available for your child."

there is some type of payoff. This may be that you feel you have to control the situation, that you feel safer not moving forward, change is scary, or that you don't deserve any better, etc.

2. Can I begin to see that all relationships take two people to exist and that I am responsible for choosing this person?

Can I see that I am at least partially responsible for the relationship not working? Can I accept that there is no blame, just responsibility?

3. Am I living in the past right now? Do I keep focusing on what happened in the past instead of choosing to move into the future?
4. Why do I believe I choose to continue to live in the past?
5. Why do I want to continue to hang onto this anger/pain?
6. Do I realize that I am the only person that can truly make me happy?
7. Do I realize that as I heal and am healthier, I am a better parent?
8. Do I want to create the best life for my child?
9. What action can I take to let my anger/pain go? What action do I need to take to be complete with this phase of this relationship?
10. What kind of life do I deserve?
11. What step can I take to move forward into my new life or to create my new life?

Know that it is so hard for your children to move on if you are not moving on. Your choosing to stay stuck in this anger and pain can be so detrimental to your children. Your child will do as well as you do. When you are upset, it causes stress for your child. When you are stuck in your anger and sadness, you are not available for your child. Your

> **"Living in the past is not the way to live. The path to freedom is to move into the future."**

child needs your love and attention. If they don't get it, they will act out or suffer in some way. If you are exhibiting this type of stuck behavior, your child will be acting out in some way. If they are not acting out now, your child will probably be feeling internal pain that will manifest in some form later in their life.

Remember that if you are still fighting about the children or not getting along, you are choosing to continue the relationship. You have either chosen the divorce or it was chosen for you. Realize that in some way you had a role in the choice. You do not have to blame yourself, just take responsibility. Make a choice now to let the anger go and choose a new life for yourself and your child. You deserve this. Choose to move into the freedom you deserve. From this place you will be able to step onto the road that will lead you to happiness and fulfillment in your life, if that is what you want. If you don't want it for you, please, I ask you to want it for your children. You will assist them in having a life of happiness and fulfillment. You will then be being the best possible parent for your child of divorce. This is the greatest gift you can give to your child.

 Read and sign the *Taking Responsibility: Living a Powerful Life* document (see Appendix). It is crucial to remember that you have a choice, this will allow you to move forward and be the best parent possible for your child.

In the next section, you will find strategies and exercises that you can use to help you find ways that you can take care of yourself, heal yourself, and grow from this experience.

Stepping Forward

Exercise 27 You may now be asking, "What can I do to move my life forward and heal this pain?" There are many ways you can support yourself in this process that I will outline below:

1. ***Enlist The Support Of Friends And Family***—Reach out to loved ones and share with them. Others are usually happy to assist you during this time. Find friends who you can talk to and who will listen to you. Make sure to remember to tell them how much you appreciate them. Make a list of names and numbers of people you will call when you are feeling down. Post the list on your refrigerator and title it "My Support List."

2. ***Monitor The Messages Of Your Internal Voice***—Or gremlin as I call it. We all have an internal voice that tells us things. A lot of times this voice comes from the past, telling us we are not good enough or did not do it right. This voice can be destructive and limit our ability to be

powerful. It is crucial to monitor what you are saying to yourself. If your gremlin is saying something negative, you have two choices. The first choice is to tell it to stop or to symbolically drown it in the sink, flush it down the toilet, etc. The second choice is to counter the negativity with something positive and affirming, like, "I am not a failure if I take risks; I am a success because I take risks." Your goal is to continue to be aware of these voices and to counter them with other positive thoughts. Often the fears that we have are not adult fears, they are the fears of a child. You must remember that you are an adult and have many more strengths and resources than you did as a child. Over time and with practice, you will become stronger than your gremlins, I know, I have taken this journey. It takes time, have patience and it does work. Shifting the message you tell yourself each day does shift your life over time.

3. *Monitor Your External Voice*—If you ever say out loud to yourself, "I am stupid." Or, "I can't believe I was that dumb," this is not healthy for you or for your children to hear. Our words create our reality and our life. We can monitor everything that comes out of our mouth. Ask yourself before speaking,

"We must have a non-violent attitude with regard to our suffering and pain. We must take care of our suffering the way we would take care of our own baby."
—Thich Nhat Hanh

will these words move my life forward or keep me stuck? Also, monitor your external conversations with others to eliminate negative speak.

4. *Allow Yourself To Grieve*—It is OK to cry. Trauma specialists know that crying helps the body release emotion and this is healthy. Honestly, the divorce may bring up and trigger a lot of old sadness. You may not only be sad for the divorce but sad for other past losses in your life. The divorce loss can be a representation of many other losses in your life. For me, I realized that a lot of the pain

I felt at the end of a relationship really had little to do with the person who left me. It was old pains and fears resurfacing, possibly from a place and time I did not even remember—possibly from my very early years as a child when I felt abandoned. Grieve, but don't allow yourself to stay stuck in that anger, hopelessness, pain and sorrow. Decide on a day or two or three-at-a-time that you will grieve if you can. Then decide on an activity that you will do to move out of the grieving space once you have grieved. One suggestion for alleviating ongoing suffering is to give yourself one hour every day, from 5–6 PM for example, to feel your grief. This is your grieving time and when the time is up, you are done. Time to get back to the present and to move forward—try this, it really works. If it's the middle of the day and you are starting to feel your emotions welling up, just postpone it until 5 PM and be done at 6 PM! For the acute pain you are feeling right after or during the divorce, it is important to allow a longer period of time for grieving, if possible. I believe you are healing old hurts right now, so give yourself this gift of time. Whatever you do, don't make yourself wrong for taking the time to heal. *The Journey from Abandonment to Healing* is a wonderful book that I mentioned earlier. It can help you better understand and move through this grief process.

5. *Be Patient*—Give yourself the time and space to heal; this is not an overnight process. Be kind to yourself right now and do good things for yourself. Think of a child who has been hurt, you would want to take care of them patiently and kindly. Treat yourself as kindly as you would want to treat your special child. You will notice an amazing phenomenon here, as you are kinder to yourself, usually you will begin to be kinder to your actual child. Thich Nhat Hanh in his book, *True Love: A Practice for Awakening the Heart*, says, "We must have a non-violent attitude with regard to our suffering and pain. We must take care of our suffering the way we would take care of our own baby."

6. *See The Positive*—Develop an attitude of gratitude. One

thing I know is that if you are reading this book, you have children. This is such an amazing gift and honor. You are so blessed to be a parent in this lifetime. Realize that you have so many wonderful things in your life. Start a gratitude journal and write each day what you are thankful for. Write down 5 things you are thankful for right now.

1. _____

2. _____

3. _____

4. _____

5. _____

Create a gratitude game with your kids where you take turns giving thanks for things in your life at least once per week. What I know is that some people seem to always see the glass half empty. If you consciously focus on what is good and positive in your life, you can change this pattern of behavior. You may have had caregivers who saw the world this way, but research has proven that we can change this. It takes practice and time but I am here to tell you that it works. This is not to say you may not have a bad day once in a while. But overall you will, more often than not, look at what you are grateful for vs. what is not good in your life. Also if you are feeling down or low, a great strategy in order to begin feeling better, is to list in your mind all the things you are grateful for. This is simple and easy and works well. I have read and believe due to seeing it happen in my own life, that if we are grateful for our blessings, we bring more good into our life. You deserve an amazing life.

7. *Create A Ritual To Symbolize The Ending Of Your Relationship*—For me, this was a letter I had written to a five-year relationship partner. I took the letter, tore it up and buried it and put a rock on it as a tombstone. This symbolized the death of the relationship for me. This ritual could also be you painting a picture or creating something to symbolize a new beginning. This could be getting

friends together for a completion ceremony to state what you are leaving behind, what you are grateful for and what you will create in your new life. This could simply be having a party with friends. You decide, but choose to do something for yourself to complete this phase of your relationship.

8. *Self-Parent*—This technique was very useful to me. In this technique, you speak to that younger child just as you would want to lovingly speak to your own child. You love that scared and wounded child so that they know you are now an adult who can take care of them. Be kind and loving to your inner child. Gabor Mate in his book suggests four things you should do as you self-parent:
    - Have compassion and curiosity, be curious, kind and patient with yourself.
    - Acceptance of self, be tolerant of your emotions, learn to not feel so guilty.
    - Do not punish yourself for where you are, know you are making gradual change and acknowledge your successes.
    - Seek guidance from a therapist or life coach, someone who can understand your behavior and help you normalize it.

9. *Travel Solo Or Take A Trip*—This can be one of the most therapeutic things to do. Decide on a place you would love to go and go there solo. I have taken many trips like this and

> **"We cannot make life easier, we can only make ourselves stronger."**
> —Vicki Lansky, author of *Divorce Book for Parents*

they are so wonderful. I always return with a stronger sense of self and with renewed happiness. Nature can also be so healing. Camping solo is one of my favorite healing activities. Nature can be a wonderful teacher if we are open to its teachings.

10. *Spirituality/Religion*—This can be whatever you consider spiritual for you. Whatever your connection is to yourself inside. This can be volunteering, giving back, attending a

church that supports you or just being in nature. I know that without all three of these I would never be where I am today. This can help you with your purpose in life and assist you to focus on something else other than your pain.

11. ***Focus On Moving Forward One Step At A Time***—As humans, we can so frequently get caught up in living in the past. Practice thinking about and living into the future each day. It is the only way to move forward. If you find yourself feeling bad about the past, stop yourself and focus into the future.

12. ***One Day At A Time***—Focus on what you need to do today; not everything you have to do for the next year. This makes life so much more manageable. Today in this world it can feel like there are so many pressures. The way to keep your pressure-level low is to focus on today and not worry about the future. As long as you are taking action on what you need to do today, the future will take care of itself.

13. ***Practice Conscious Breathing***—For one minute, three times a day, breathe in for four seconds, hold for seven seconds and then exhale for eight seconds. You can also just consciously focus on deep breathing for a minute during the day at various times. This will bring you into the present moment and this is the only place where we are free from pain. There is no suffering in the present moment. We are suffering for the past or the future. Focus on your breathing in this moment, suffering does not exist here, only quiet relaxation. Breathing consciously is our easiest access to lowering our stress and anxiety level.

14. ***Learn To Meditate***—It quiets the mind. Meditation is cited by many health and wellness experts as a way to relieve stress. Meditation CDs that I recommend are by Jon Kabat-Zin PhD and were developed in conjunction with the University of Massachusetts Medical School. Meditation helps us return to our strong self with which I believe we were born. We reconnect with ourselves through meditation and this is one of the most healing things we can do. Our path to health is truly all inside of

us. These CDs can be purchased from my website at www. healthychildrenofdivorce.com.

15. *Take Care Of Yourself And Do Your Healing Work*—This can take many forms but one important aspect is to nutritionally take care of your body. Eating well is critical. Another aspect is to exercise and physically take care of your body. There are also so many other healing options available, such as *reiki*, healing touch, acupuncture, yoga, journaling, EMDR, cranial sacral therapy and massage. Volunteering also can be very healing for individuals—at schools, homes for the elderly, homeless shelters, animal shelters, or other helping agencies. Whatever feels healthy for you is what you should do.

16. *Remember, You Are A Beginner*—Beginners take baby steps and sometimes fall down. Just as you did when you were a baby learning to walk, you may fall down during this journey. Give yourself room to make mistakes, it is OK. As long as you intend to move forward, that is what is important. Give yourself credit for taking positive actions, such as reading this book. Change can be slow but if you are committed and practice, you will continuously improve. I encourage you to not give up if it feels challenging. Trust that you are making progress. You did not yell at your child when they were learning to walk and fell, so don't yell at yourself. Give yourself encouragement and love through this process.

17. *Goals: Set Goals For Your Life, Write Them Down*— This works. What are two goals you want to set right now? These could be small, simple goals such as: take a 10-minute walk today or bigger ones, such as: walk three times per week or exercise three times per week. Set two goals right now that you want to focus on in the next week.

    1. _____

    2. _____

18. *Tell Yourself You Are Doing A Great Job*—Make sure you remember to do this, especially if you are reading this book—hooray for you!!!! You are awesome!!! I truly mean

this from the bottom of my heart because if you are reading this, you are a parent who is concerned about your child. You are a good parent, no matter what has happened in your past. You have the ability to create a wonderful new future.

I honestly ask you to heal your pain so your child can heal. When you are healthy, your child can be healthy. This will play a role in allowing your child to have a future as a healthy adult. Children are dependent upon adults for nurturing and guidance. Please take care of yourself so you can best support and take care of your child. Your child's chance of growing into a happy, healthy adult is directly related to your ability to heal your own pain and live a happy, healthy life. Choose this for you and choose this for your child. You both deserve it.

Questions For Reflection:

What do I need to do to take care of me?

_____

_____

_____

_____

What is special about me?

_____

_____

_____

Why do I deserve a good life?

_____

_____

_____

_____

_____

_____

_____

_____

_____

_____

_____

_____

_____

~~7~~

Fatal Mistake #6: The Dating Game—Not Playing Fair And Not Following The Rules

How Dating Can Cause Stress For Your Child

The truth about dating is that it can cause stress for your children. You impact their level of stress by your actions. Questions about dating arise in every session of "Co-Parenting Through Your Divorce" I facilitate. It is my view that parents must do all things possible to mitigate the effects of the divorce on their children. One easy way to do this is to be conscious of your dating. Dating done wrong has the potential to cause stress for children for three crucial reasons, and they are important to understand.

To The Child, Parent Dating Signifies The End Of The Marriage Relationship

The first reason parental dating causes stress for children is that dating signifies to children the end of their parents' marriage relationship. Children usually fantasize that their parents will reunite. Once children are aware that a parent is beginning a new relationship and that someone else is coming into the picture, they know that probably there is no hope of their parents reconciling and reuniting. This realization can be stressful and can cause sadness, fear and/or anger for children. I heard from a therapist colleague whose college-aged client was a child of divorce, and after 10 years, this now grown adult was still hoping his parents would get back together. It is recommended to wait one year after the official separation to begin dating (see end of this chapter for more information).

Children May Feel Jealous Of This New Person

When you begin dating, the second reason children of divorce feel stress is that they may feel jealous. They may not want to share your time together with a new "outsider." This is especially true if they only see you for visits on weekends or it is early in your divorce/separation process. It can feel scary for kids to have to "get along" with this new person. Your child may feel threatened by this other person, they may fear this person will hurt you or take you away from them. This is a very common fear for children.

I want parents to also understand that sometimes kids just pretend to like your new partner because they know it will make you happy. Do not force anyone on your children. If you do begin dating someone, slowly introduce them. Do not make your child feel like they are in competition with your dating partner for your time and attention. I remember when my dad first started dating my step-mom. He told us, "Judy is going to Canada fishing with us." I thought I was going to faint. Fishing in Canada had always been a dad-and-his-girls trip. At that point, I had hardly spent time with Judy because she met my dad when I was 22. I told my dad that if she went, I was not going. It was nothing against Judy, whom I love now; I just wanted that quality time with my dad. Just so you know it is common, my sister felt the same way!

You should explain to your child that there are many kinds of love. The kind of love a parent has for their child will always be there, no matter who else comes into the picture. Your child was there first, therefore, they will always be first. Let them know that you as a parent need to have friends and other people in your life; this makes you happy. However, the love you feel for your child is a very different and special kind of love that you will never feel for another adult.

The Other Parent's Anger And Jealousy

The third reason your dating can cause stress for your children, which can sometimes be very emotionally damaging, is the anger or upset their other parent displays now that you are dating. Parents make children feel guilty that they are spending time with their other parent and someone new. Parents make it known that they have great disdain for this other woman or other man. It is the parent's own jealousy that drives this behavior but it negatively impacts your child. The child cannot even discuss their time with you because if they mention the new person in their mother or father's life, it sets their other parent off. They may feel guilty that they are spending time with this other person. Once again, this is another good reason to hold off on introducing a new person too early.

In order to mitigate the negative impact of your dating on your children, I have created the Divorce Dating Game Rules below. I also have included a dating questionnaire that you can answer prior to introducing any partner to your child. It can be found at the end of this chapter. Dating is a piece of this divorce puzzle that IS in your complete control. Choose to do it well for your child. It will be best for everyone involved, including your new partner and your relationship together.

The Divorce Dating Game Rules

Rule #1: You Are Always Their Parent First

The first thing to remember is that you had your children first and you chose them, so you must always put them first. Your children need you during this crucial time especially during and immediately following your divorce/separation. When you seek out a potential dating partner, the new person must also understand this fact. The fact is that you are always a parent first; a new dating partner will truly never be first. If your children need you, you will be there for them no matter what. Sometimes people who date parents of children feel jealous of the kids. This is important for you to recognize, because there should be no contest. If you sense your dating partner is becoming jealous of your relationship with your kids, it is so crucial to have an honest, open conversation with them. If they are not able to allow you to put your kids first, they are not the right person for you to be dating at this point. If you care that much about them, then date them once your kids are 18 and you have less responsibility! Your dating partner must also be able to put your children's needs first.

My stepmother, Judy, was able to do this. If she attended one of our events, my mom could not handle it and there was so much craziness. Judy was willing to skip events initially because she knew my mom's reaction to her attendance caused us pain and stress. Judy gave our family some space initially. I do not advocate accommodating a parent that acts inappropriately, as you do not want to enable their negative behavior. I am saying that in our extreme situation, I saw our stepmom put her step-kids' needs first. By the way, they get along fine now; it takes time. If my family could do this, so can yours. If you are the parent that is causing this type of stress for your family, you need assistance to get healthy. This behavior is not acceptable and is not fair to your children.

Rule #2: Don't Pretend A Partner Is Your Friend

Guess what mom and dad? You have raised really intelligent children—kids know. They know intuitively if something is going on between two adults that is more than friendship. I worked with one child whose mom said that she was not introducing her boyfriend to her children as a boyfriend, only as a friend. Meeting this "friend," who was introduced to this boy by his mom in a very casual environment, created this reaction from the 7-year old I was working with:

> *"What if my mom marries this guy? What if they get a divorce and we have to go through this again? What about my dad? He will be alone."*

This child was only aware of his parents' final decision to divorce for 4–5 months but he already had these fears about his mother's new relationship. These are actual fears that kids can have.

Rule #3: Take Time For YOU Before Dating!

Children's adjustment to divorce is directly related to their parents' adjustment. Be sure to do your "adjusting work" first, which may mean counseling or coaching to look at yourself and your role in the divorce. It is important to understand what actually happened in your relationship/divorce situation. Whatever you do, please do not just jump into something to avoid being alone. Take time for yourself to really assess if you are healthy enough for new relationship. Do this for you and your children. Healthy parents create healthy children. For myself, after a long-term relationship break-up, initially I blamed the other person. When I took some time with myself alone, I was able to acknowledge and see my role in why the relationship did not work.

The statistics tell us that the failure rate of second marriages is higher than the failure rate of first marriages (60% of second marriages fail). If we do not assess our role in the past break-up, we are very likely to choose another partner that also may not honor our needs and this marriage may also end in divorce. As you can imagine, it can be devastating for children to have to go through this loss process twice. Taking time for you to heal is one of the best possible ways to avoid a second divorce. Do this for yourself and your child. This is discussed in detail in Chapter 6: Choosing Not to Heal Your Pain.

Rule #4: Please... Take Time For Your Children

It is common that parents want to introduce a new dating partner to children. You want your children to meet the person that is now sharing your life and time. Remember that for your child, this may NOT be an exciting event. They may not share your enthusiasm for this person. In fact, they may see this person as a threat and an intrusion into their time with you. Remember that especially if you are sharing custody with their other parent, your child needs good quality time with you solo. Quality time with you one-on-one is most important for that first year while children are adjusting to the divorce/separation.

As I write this, a friend passed away unexpectedly at the young age of 35. He was an amazing man and lived life fully and with integrity. He had a quality life. I am once again reminded that it is not the quantity of time we spend here but the quality of it that matters. Choose to spend quality time with your children, it may be one of the most important things you ever do. You will never regret it. At the end of your life, you will never have to say, "I wish I had spent more quality time with my children." When you invite someone you are dating to spend time with you and your children early in the divorce process, it is not honoring your child's time with you. They need your full attention during this transition in their lives. Your attention will undoubtedly be distracted and your children will notice. Take time to know this person separate from your child to make sure they are a good fit for you. If this person is not OK with that, this is not the relationship for you.

I recently worked with an 11-year-old boy who did not like his dad's girlfriend so he was not visiting his father. He asked his father if the two of them could go to dinner by themselves one night a week. The father's response was, "I do everything with my girlfriend." This made my client feel very sad. This is an example of misplaced priorities and how not to treat your child. This father's response creates a lasting feeling of not being loved in a child. Your child needs to come first.

Rule #5: Evaluate The Future Of This Dating Relationship

There are things you can actually do to ensure this relationship is one you consider solid for the future. First, ask yourself if this person is someone you can see yourself creating a future with? Can you see this person with your children long term? Does this person adequately fulfill your needs, wants and desires in a relationship? Is this person stable enough to bring your family into their life and maintain balance? Is this person stable enough to effectively deal with the sometimes added stress of a stepfamily? Ask your new partner if they want the relationship to continue into the future. The biggest mistake you can make is introducing someone to your children who may not be around for long. Be realistic about this, answer my questionnaire at the end of this chapter honestly and don't introduce someone until you have all of those details worked out. The main reason for this is that if your children begin to like your new partner and this relationship does not work out, they are left to deal with another loss that was totally unnecessary. I realize that sometimes relationships will end, however, if you take all the steps I suggest, you will have done all you can to act in the best interest of your child. It is completely not fair to your child to introduce them early on to someone and then rip that person out of their life.

Rule #6: Location, Location, Location—What Is This Potential Partner's Location Or Future Location?

It is vital for children to grow up near both parents if possible. This is the best way to ensure that both parents spend adequate time with their children. Consider where this potential partner lives currently or where they want to live in the future. Will this be near your children's other parent? Near means within a reasonable driving distance. Depending on your custody situation, you will need to ask yourself different questions. If your relationship with your ex-spouse is not healthy, will this person support staying in the same area with this person, even if it may be easier to move away from them? I have seen parents move far distances away from their children because it feels easier for them. When I say far, I mean distances that are too far to reasonably drive for the parents to exchange their children. This would be different for each family but it would be more than a 2-hour drive for most families. The ultimate test of whether it is too far away is if you can't see your children as often as you used to. I know parents who have moved thousands of miles away after getting a divorce. This is a selfish thing to do. Moving away from your children should not be an option and should be considered only in the most extenuating circumstances.

Rule #7: Ensure This Is A Healthy Person For Your Children

First consider, is this person completely healthy for you? Do you feel calm with them, do they compliment you or do you spend a lot of time arguing and being upset with them? Have you seen this person with other children? Does this person express a true interest in children? Have you asked them how they feel about being a possible stepparent for your children? If this person has their own children, are they a great parent for them? Do you have a similar philosophy regarding raising children? Will this person be respectful of your former spouse in front of your children? These questions should all be answered **before** introducing a new person to your children. If you can't answer them, then it is not time yet to introduce them to your children. Your children deserve the best and the best is that you are clear on all of these issues prior to introducing them to someone else.

Rule #8: Tell Children You Intend To Date

After you are separated and/or divorced for a period of time (at least 3 to 6 months), it is fine to begin communicating about the dating process by initially telling your child that you plan to date at some point in the future—it is recommended you wait a year after your child is aware of your separation/ divorce to begin dating. If possible, you should not be actually dating yet. You are just preparing your child for when the time comes. Make sure to tell them they will always be first and that you love them. Tell them you will let them know when this time comes but that you are not dating right now.

Rule #9: Introduce In Steps

If you feel this is the right time to introduce your dating partner to your child, it is important to do this in at least three steps. First, introduce your child to your dating partner in an informal setting. This could be at a park or playground, at an event where others are present, or at an outdoor event. Your child should be allowed to meet your new dating partner without any forced conversation. Let your child know prior to this first meeting that this is your friend and you are dating them. Second, do activities together and just spend time with your child and your dating partner. However, always remember that especially if you share custody with your child's co-parent that your dating partner should not be present during most of your time with your child. You should see your dating partner when you do not have your child, especially if you have less than 50% custody of your child. You must continue to spend one-on-one time with your children. Third, after your child and dating partner have spent considerable time together with you, they can now possibly spend some time alone together (if your child requests this or it is necessary due to circumstances). You must ensure that your child feels very comfortable with this and that you have witnessed your child and your dating partner interacting well together on several occasions before this should happen. It is difficult to put a time frame on this (due to all the variables in different families) but 3–6 months seems the minimum amount of time that your child should spend with you and your dating partner together before they are ever solo with this person.

In summary, children are our future, let's all agree to treat them with the love, respect and caring that they deserve, especially during the dating after separation/divorce process. This includes taking care of yourself, making sure that you spend quality one-on-one time with your children, and ensuring that all potential dating partners will be good role models for your children.

Questions To Ask Prior To Introducing Your Children To Your Dating Partner

1. Does my dating partner know and understand that I am always a parent first?
2. Does this person like children?
3. Have I seen this person interacting positively with children?
4. Do I believe this person would be a positive role model for my child?
5. Would I want this person to be a potential influence in my child's life?
6. Have I dated this person for at least three to six months or feel fully committed to this person and they to me?
7. Is this a person I could see myself committing to long term?
8. Have I had a discussion with this person about our possible future together?
9. Do I know that this person would agree to be a part of my family with my children?
10. Does this dating partner approve of and understand my current relationship/situation with my child's other parent?

11. Will I still be able to fulfill my parenting time commitments if I date this person? If I live in the same area as my child's other parent, does the person I am dating want to stay in the same location or live in this location (within driving distance)? If they live somewhere else that would limit my time with my child if I moved there, are they willing to move to the general area where my children are?

12. Have I been divorced or in my child's mind officially separated (the date your child knew their parents were no longer living together and you told them about the divorce) for at least a year?

13. Do I truly believe in my heart that my child/children are emotionally ready to be introduced to someone else?

If you answered *No* to any of the above questions, you are not yet ready to introduce your child to the person you are dating. If you don't feel ready to discuss these questions with your dating partner, you also are not ready to introduce your child to the person you are dating. Take your time; it is important to proceed with confidence in your choices. Always remember that you are a parent first. Your children will thank you for putting them first.

Questions For Reflection:

Am I really read to date right now?

_____

_____

_____

_____

What do I want and need in my next partner?

_____

_____

_____

_____

If I am dating, what are the healthy and unhealthy aspects of the relationship, especially as they relate to my children?

_____

_____

_____

_____

_____

_____

_____

_____

_____

_____

_____

_____

~~8~~

Fatal Mistake #7: Checking Out On Your Children

Recently, I spoke with a former co-worker. He was going through a divorce and was telling me that he now lives in New York. He and his family had been living in Iowa and his daughters were still there. He has three younger daughters ages 1 and 3, and an older daughter, age 13, from a prior marriage. I could not wrap my mind around the concept that he had left his three beautiful daughters in Iowa and moved to New York. I cannot even begin to imagine the stories that his daughters are thinking now or will feel and think in the future about why their father left them. Your children need you more than ever during this time in their lives. They need your physical presence to help them feel safe and secure during this time. Feeling secure is a basic need of children that allows them to develop appropriately. Not having the amazing experience of seeing your children grow up and providing them support to become the most amazing people possible seems unimaginable to me. You chose to be a parent, even if the pregnancy itself was not planned. You knew the potential ramifications of your actions. It's not a job you get to quit. If you quit the most important job in your life, you are giving up on your children and yourself. Even if you are not considering leaving your child, please continue to read this chapter and do the exercises. They will assist you in being the best parent you can be. If you are considering leaving your children, please read this chapter and consider staying. Your children need you.

You may be saying, "I have some good reasons for doing this." I am guessing that some of these reasons could even be subconscious beliefs you have about yourself and your ability to parent your children. Let's explore the reasons you may be using to justify leaving your children or being an absent parent.

Reason #1: The Story You May Be Telling Yourself: "I Am Not A Good Parent"

As I was writing this, I wondered why a parent would choose not to be with his or her children as they grew up? After working with many parents, my belief is, whether you know it consciously or not, your reason could be: "I am not a good parent," or some other version of this story, such as, "My parents were bad parents; how could I do a good job?". I believe that even if you are consciously using another reason for leaving your children, that in the majority of cases, reason number one ("I am not a good parent") may be underlying the conscious reason you give. I want to share with you some good news—whatever your situation is, you can get assistance to be a better parent. I want you to know that your children love you very much, no matter what has happened. Children are the most forgiving creatures on earth. They want you in their lives. In some cases they may not be saying that right now and may have some anger to work through. If they are pushing you away, know it's because they are hurting. The best thing you can do for them and your relationship is to stay and to continue to love them. You may want to enroll in counseling together. Remaining in your child's life will help them feel safe and secure and learn to trust you over time.

 Read the sentence below and listen to what you hear in your mind after you read the statement:

I Am A Good Parent.

What thoughts came to your mind upon reading this statement? What do you tell yourself about being a parent? What do you feel about your ability to be a good parent? Maybe your co-parent has even labeled you as being a bad parent and this story sticks with you. Maybe you had bad parents, so how could you be a good parent? Write your thoughts below about the statement above:

_____

_____

_____

If you have negative stories, these stories you tell yourself must be transformed into positive ones, even if right now you don't believe them. Next, I would like you to write on the lines below five reasons that you are a good parent. It is important to write them. The first one can be, "I love my child(ren)." Please do this exercise whether or not you are in your child's life.

Why I feel I am a good parent:

_____

_____

_____

Now write your answers to the question below (this could include classes, books, or any other things you could do for your child such as communicating with them frequently, telling them you love them, giving them a hug, volunteering at their school or asking for their forgiveness):

What can I do to be an even better parent?

_____

_____

_____

Exercise 30: If you even slightly believe your story about not being a good parent, I would like you to write out why you *are* a good parent once a day for the next two weeks.

1. Why I (your name here) _____ am a good parent is (this answer can be different each time you write it):

   _____

   _____

   _____

2. Write this sentence (filling in the blank with why you are a good parent) ten times each day for two weeks. This is a way to change your old belief systems and to help you to begin to believe you are a good parent. If you believe

it, you will be closer to being it. If this is really challenging for you, I recommend you see a professional or take some actions to improve your parenting skills. My website has resources www.healthychildrenofdivorce.com. Your children deserve a parent who believes he or she is a good parent.

3. Take five minutes and ask your child why you are a good parent and how you could be an even better parent.

Your children may have the best answers. After canoeing all day with my four-, five- and six-year-old cousins, I asked them why I should have children. Their response was, "Because you are nice to kids and we had fun." Have this dialogue with your children so they know you care about how you are doing as a parent. You also are letting them know you value their opinions, feelings and thoughts. You may be very positively surprised at the answers you hear. Compare your answers with your children's answers.

Reason #2: I Have Made Too Many Mistakes

Maybe you have made some mistakes as a parent. All parents have; and I want to repeat what I shared earlier — children are some of the most forgiving beings on this earth. Children are much more forgiving than adults. I worked with a boy who had been abandoned by his drug abusing mother. His mother had been in and out of prison seven times. The son had been placed in various county out-of-home placements. Mom worked hard and got her son back after three years of good behavior. This resilient and remarkable boy was able to forgive his mother and move forward by working together in therapy.

You can ask your children for forgiveness. Tell them how you are committed to doing it differently in the future. You can say something like, "I am sorry for not calling on Wednesday. I commit that I will put it on my schedule so that I remember to call every Wednesday in the future." Kids understand that we all make mistakes, however, don't ask for forgiveness until you have a plan in place to help ensure this mistake does not happen again. You have to decide what behaviors you can commit to change for your child. The kids I have worked with are so amazing. They have so much love for the adults in their lives. Children's ability to love and forgive feels nothing short of a miracle to me. If your child deserves an apology and a commitment from you to change, please, give them that gift.

Reason #3: My Child's Other Parent Is Too Unreasonable; It's Best For My Child If I Stay Away

This is absolutely not true. Your problems with your child's other parent or guardian have nothing to do with your time with your child. What is best for your child is for both parents to be involved in their life. If you choose to stay away from your child due to ongoing conflict with their other parent, you are in effect punishing your child. You are also reinforcing the behavior of the other parent, who may want you to NOT see your child! We know that when we reinforce bad behavior, it continues to happen. Treat your unreasonable co-parent as you would your child, do not reinforce their bad behavior.

Your goal is to find ways not to involve your child in the conflict. You can arrange pick ups and drop offs at neutral sites, such as a family member's home or a professional agency that specializes in this for families. If your child is school aged or in daycare, a great arrangement is for one parent to drop them off and the other parent to pick them up after school—just be sure to inform the school that this is your arrangement. This way, you do not have to have contact with the other parent. If it is so challenging that you cannot reason with the other parent, use a mediator or a parenting coordinator. These professionals are trained to assist your family in making decisions in your child's best interest. If you need to have drop-offs professionally monitored, there are organizations that offer this service. If you want to find out more about this service in your city, this is called a monitored exchange.

You can also find other creative ways to connect with your child through email, voice mails, cell phones when appropriate, or texting. If your child is school age or in preschool/daycare, see if you can volunteer at their school. Get a school calendar so you can attend their events. Many children today are on Facebook, MySpace or some other on-line social forum. These websites can provide you with important information regarding your child's activities.

If you are a parent that is court-ordered to see your child only under supervision, I know this can feel especially challenging. This is called parenting time or supervised visitation in most states. In this case, you sometimes have to pay money to be supervised to see your child. Remember that the relationship with your child is priceless. Even in a supervised setting, you can continue to build your relationship with your child. I worked at a supervised visitation center and one dad had been coming faithfully to see his three children for years. Those children developed a good relationship with their father and you could tell they loved him very much. They knew their dad loved them enough to do whatever he had to do to see them, and that was what mattered. In these situations it is so important to remember that it is not the quantity of time with your children but the quality of the time you spend with them.

Reason #4: My New Family And I Will Have An Easier Start If I Live Far Away From My Unreasonable Ex

I really doubt that anyone ever admits to this actually happening but I have seen it with my own eyes. This is running away from your problems and not accepting responsibility for your life. Remember, you are always a parent to your children first. Your new spouse is second when it comes to doing what is in the best interests of your children. Your children were part of your life first; they deserve to be put first. They are children; they need you. It may feel to you at times that the easy way would be to put your new family first. I don't doubt that this could feel like the easier option for you. I am guessing that if you have a difficult ex, that your new spouse or partner may very much be in favor of moving far away from this person and your children. I have something really crucial to tell you, and this is important for you to understand:

This is the easy way out for you;
this is absolutely the hardest
and most painful way for your child.

Mary, Max, And Mitchell's Story

A former coworker of mine had recently married a woman that had three children from her previous marriage. The children were aged three-, five-, and eight-years old. My coworker barraged me with countless stories of how terrible the children's father was, telling the children lies and putting them in the middle. The children came to our office once with their mom to visit my co-worker. They followed mom around in complete love. They also loved their future step-dad, or at least they knew their mom wanted them to love him, so they did. Imagine my complete bewilderment when about a year later my co-worker shared that he and his new wife were moving four states away.

I asked him, "What will the children do?"

He responded, "Stay here [in Tennessee] with their dad."

To me, this was the absolute worst option for the children. It was worse than any of the stories I had heard about this previously terrible dad. Were they really going to leave the children in the care of "a known crazy man" as he had been described to me? I could not imagine a worse scenario for these children's long-term physical and emotional health. If what my co-worker had said was true about the children's father, these children needed the presence of their mother even more. Many children in this situation where one parent moves a significant distance away, come to feel that their parent has abandoned them.

Being the egocentric beings that they are (children are by nature the center of their own universes), each of them in their own way will most likely believe that in part, their mother's leaving was their fault. This will impact them for the rest of their lives. The last time I heard from my former colleague, they had just had their first child and still lived four states away from her children. My email reply to him was:

"How are her children in Tennessee doing?" I never got a

response to that question.

Children also feel abandoned if a parent chooses a new partner over them. In the case of my friend, Sue, her father's new wife did not like children, so her father opted not to have much contact with his children after remarrying. Sue now deals with a lot of abandonment issues as an adult. Intimate relationships have been challenging for her.

We all must make choices in our lives and if we have children our responsibility is to make choices that are in their best interest. When you became a parent, I believe you signed up for that responsibility. I also had another father in one of my divorce education classes who admitted that he had decided to limit contact with his daughter because

"In the case of my friend, Sue, her father's new wife did not like children, so her father opted not to have much contact with his children after remarrying. Sue now deals with a lot of abandonment issues as an adult. Intimate relationships have been challenging for her."

he thought it would be "easier for her." He was in constant conflict with her mother. He thought it was in his daughter's best interest that he stay away due to the terrible conflict. His daughter was a teenager and after about six months of very limited contact, she emailed him and asked, "Dad, why don't you love me anymore?" He realized that his daughter had no understanding of why he had pulled away. For all he knew, her mother had told her some terrible story; it does happen. It is best to communicate with your child so you know their concerns. During my class, this father made the commitment to not allow his relationship with his child's other parent to dictate his relationship with his child. If you allow this, you are giving the other parent complete control, which is probably their goal. Also if the other parent is still angry and exhibiting this type of behavior, your child needs you even more to be a strong presence in their life. Your job is to take steps to minimize communication with the other parent and seek out a professional to assist you and your co-parent in making parenting decisions.

Remember you chose to have your children, please continue to choose them. They will be adults before you can blink your eyes. I can tell you that adults are much less forgiving than children. I hope no one ever told you that being a parent would be an easy job. If they did, they were wrong! Sometimes the most amazing things in life were the most difficult at one point in our lives. Don't check out on your children, check into their lives. They need you.

The Parent Left Standing—What To Tell Your Child If Their Other Parent Checks Out

There are many different scenarios where parents leave the life of their child. One scenario I have dealt with in my practice was a mother who left her 2-1/2-year-old son in the care of the girl's father while she left the state due to drug use and another pregnancy. This mother had been a good mother and had been very involved in her son's life prior to this time. The boy's father, who was not sure when or if his son's mom would return, said the following to their young son:

- Your mom loves you.
- She is sick and has to take care of herself to get better.
- I am here for you and love you very much.

If a parent is in prison, one method I have used to tell the child is that the parent is learning to be a better parent and person, which is hopefully true. If you are not sure where and when the parent may return, you can say the following:

- I know your parent loves you (all parents love their kids). Do not say negative things about the other parent, you will only hurt your child.
- Parenting is a big job and parents sometimes are afraid they will make a mistake so they go away because they are scared they will fail at being a parent. It has nothing to do with you. You are a great kid. Your parent loves you.

- Your parent still cares about you.
- Remember the good things about mom/dad? If possible, talk about these things with your child and the happy memories they have with their other parent.
- If you think this is true: your parent is getting help right now because they are sick.
- Mom/dad has made some poor choices but she is a good person inside, this good place is the place you came from. You can make different choices than your mom/dad.[51]
- How are you feeling?

Ideas to help your child get through this:

- Have your child write a letter to or draw a picture for the other parent if they are upset or sad or have a happy event they want to share with the other parent. Tell them they can give this to their parent when they see them again. I suggest a mom or dad box that they put the letters in.
- Have your child see a counselor to help them process this event in a healthy way.
- Tell your child how much you love them and how happy you are that they are in your life. Tell them you are here to stay forever.
- Remind the child of the good times they've had and how much their other parent loves them.
- Find another role model, preferably the same sex as the missing parent, and ask this person to play a positive role in your child's life. This can be a family member or close friend. Big Brothers/ Big Sisters is also a very good option.
- Remind your child of their positive qualities and their strengths frequently.

Checking Out On Your Child By Moving Them Away

In some cases, I have seen parents want to move their children away from the child's other parent. They usually think this will make everyone's lives easier, but it is not easier for their child. There are many factors and considerations to this decision and it would be best to weigh pros and cons with a professional. I believe that moving the child away from their other parent should be done in only the most extreme circumstances, however there are some circumstances that may warrant it and work for all parties involved. If you have been living in the same area for many years and now that you are divorcing you want to move, it is an unfair expectation to think the other parent should move to where you want to move. It is also unfair to your children to move them away from their other parent.

> **"The collective evidence suggests that frequent and predictable contact with the non-custodial parent is beneficial for children."**
> —Nicolas Long, PhD and Rex Forehand, PhD

The Parent Who Wants To Re-Enter Your Child's Life: What To Tell The Re-Entering Parent

Research tells us again and again that children benefit from having some type of relationship with both of their parents. Most children would rather have any type of relationship than no relationship at all.[52] It is important for you to remember this because your anger at your child's other parent can sometimes make you not want this person to re-enter your child's life. In the example above, since mom just up and left one day, dad did not trust she was going to return in a consistent manner. I worked with this family as a parenting coordinator to help build this trust back. The important questions you need to discuss with the parent that wants to reenter your child's life are the following:

1. Is this parent willing to make a long-term commitment to your child? The other parent needs to give their word to you that they are committed to being involved for the rest of your child's life. Your child does not need someone they love coming in and out of their lives erratically. I recommend putting in writing how often they will see your child and have them sign it.

2. Is this parent willing to gradually re-enter your child's life? It is healthiest for your child to gradually have increased time with the other parent. This may take many different forms and it would be best to seek professional advice from someone who specializes in this area to ensure the best schedule is worked out for your child.

3. Is this parent willing to spend time alone with your child initially, without other relatives or new partners? My recommendation is that they spend time solo with their children for at least the first six months to build back the relationship between the two of them.

4. The other parent should be willing to attend therapy, at their expense, with your child to help rebuild this relationship.

5. If it has been a long period of parental absence or other extenuating circumstances, the other parent should be willing to consult with a third-party therapist specializing in attachment and reintegration. It is in your child's and the other parent's best interest to do this right and to reestablish a healthy bond between the two of them.

If the other parent can agree to all of the above, then it would be in your child's best interest to have contact with the other parent. If this is handled in a healthy manner, it will impact your child positively. They will know they are loved by both parents, and for children, this is so important for healthy growth and development.

Questions for Reflection:

If I have checked out on my child, how can I check back in?

_____

_____

_____

_____

_____

If I am the custodial parent of my child, what can I do to positively promote my child's relationship with their other parent (if this is possible).

_____

_____

_____

_____

_____

_____

_____

_____

_____

_____

_____

_____

_____

_____

_____

_____

_____

~~9~~

Strategies For Effective Parenting After Divorce: Staying Connected To And Meeting The Needs Of Your Child

Your child needs you more than ever during this time. They need you to be connected with them and they need you to be the best parent possible. I know that all parents want to be the best parent they can be for their child. This chapter provides strategies that will assist you in reaching this goal.

Effective-Parenting Strategy #1: Staying Connected Even When Apart

There are numerous avenues available to you to remain connected to your child and a part of their life. You may not be with your child as much as you want, and if this is true for you, some of the ideas below may be helpful. One of my co-facilitators of the class *Co-Parenting Through Your Divorce* tells that he did a lot of extra-curricular activities to remain in his child's life even when he did not have that much parenting time with his child. This kept him close to his child even with limited one-on-one parenting time. Whether your child is far away or close by, these ideas will help you both feel more connected:

Options To Have More Connection To Your Child If You Live Close

- Coaching their sports teams
- Volunteer with their school's PTA
- Volunteer at School
- Volunteer to chaperone school events

Options To Have More Connection To Your Child If You Live Far Away (These Can Also Work If You Live Close Or Have Limited Access To Your Kids)

- Read age-appropriate books separately and discuss
- Make and share videos
- Fax/email
- Pictures
- Skype video
- Instant messaging (this is pretty neat, I just tried it myself), have your children teach you!
- Tape record a book or stories for your child so your child can listen to you reading to them at night. You can also just send messages to older children.

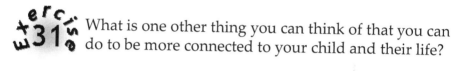 What is one other thing you can think of that you can do to be more connected to your child and their life?

_____

_____

Effective-Parenting Strategy #2: Develop New Traditions

Children love traditions, big and small. Nineteen years after leaving my family's home, I still love to get fish fry on Friday nights because that is something that my family did many Friday nights as I was growing up. It was a happy time because the workweek was done and Mom did not have to cook! Halloween is one of my favorite times because every year I would get dressed up and we would go to my Grandma and Grandpa's; it was so fun! Halloween is still my favorite holiday.

It is time to think about what you want your new family to look like. In this new family, you can create new traditions with your children. Ask your children what traditions they enjoy from your past family that they want to continue. Make sure that between the two co-parents, you carry on these traditions when possible. Please, avoid fighting about who gets what holiday or event. Just know that as long as your child is able to participate in the traditions, they will be happy. Take this opportunity to develop traditions you may not have been able to engage in when you were married. After my parents divorced, my dad and sisters always went and cut their own Christmas tree for dad's house. My mom has asthma so we could never have a real tree in our home when my parents were together. Together, my dad and sisters created a new tradition for their new family.

Think about the things you would like to do and then create traditions for you and your kids around them. One colleague of mine said his kids always bring up the times that they went camping. He said he really did not have much money but it was a tradition so they did it every year without fail. His children, who are now older, bring it up as one of their most fun memories. Of course, children have the best memories if they have fun while doing the activities. Other cost-effective ideas are game night, pizza night, movie night, etc.

Effective-Parenting Strategy #3: Use Positive Feedback Techniques

Your child thrives when they feel that you love them and recognize their positive behaviors. I cannot stress to you how important this is. I believe that as adults we get into a habit of seeing what is wrong in the world. We look for problems. We get rewarded in our jobs for seeing what is wrong that could impact our organization—we get paid for thinking critically. This type of thinking does not work well with children. Children's self esteem is directly related to the type of feedback and or praise they receive from their parents. If you give your child a lot of positive feedback and positively interact with them, they will have higher self esteem.

> **"If you give your child a lot of positive feedback and positively interact with them, they will have higher self esteem."**

This is a simple fact. For some adults, being critical with themselves and others is a way of being. This can begin with our caregivers being critical with us. Parental depression and anger can also negatively impact children in this same way. If as parents, we are depressed or angry and see everything as difficult and bad, this is what we teach our children. They begin to look for what is bad in themselves and in the world. This is also referred to as judging. If we are judging others, we are usually judging ourselves and our children.

Recently, I read Marilee Adams' book, *Change Your Questions, Change Your Life*. Adams describes how every time we look at someone or something, we typically ask ourselves questions. We ask ourselves questions our entire life. Too often, the questions usually are something like:

- What is wrong here?
- What did I/they do wrong?
- Why can't I do this?
- What negative thing could happen?
- What if I don't do this?

I assert that we can also have judging thoughts like:

- Wow, that guy has bad hair
- That person can never do it right
- That lady is ugly
- I am fat

We can also have many subconscious beliefs running in our mind like:

- I can't do this right
- I am not right
- No one can be trusted
- I must protect myself
- I am not good enough

And many, many more....

Adams explains that if we can teach ourselves to change the typically negative tone of our questions into positive ones, then we can change our entire outlook. If you change your question from "Why can't I do this?", which leaves you hopeless and accepting defeat, to "What can I do about this?", you give yourself options. With options, you are empowered to make a change. Adams' book helped me begin to really manage my thoughts and words.

As I was practicing her technique to change the questions in my life, I was also working with children and families. I realized that this is a great tool for parenting. Instead of seeing what your child is doing wrong, see what they are doing right and recognize them for this. Over time, they will do less and less of the bad and more and more of the good stuff. This is called positive reinforcement. The other amazing benefit of this is that your child will also begin to look for what is right. They will see what is right in themselves vs. what is wrong. This is a lifelong gift you can give your child.

Four Steps To Change Your Questions

1. Be aware of the beliefs and thoughts running through your mind. Begin to notice when you are thinking negatively. You must make this a very conscious effort because we so automatically do this. This can be a very old habit and may be a challenge to break. It may take a bit of time.
2. Once you notice that the negative thought is there, ask yourself a different positive question. Ask yourself, what is good here, what did I do well today, what is good about that person? Sometimes, I will say the word *love* over and over to break a negative thought.
3. Practice this over and over again until your thoughts begin to change. It took many years for these patterns to develop so give yourself time to recreate these questions and patterns of thinking.
4. Be aware of the words you are speaking as well and ensure that you are verbalizing only positive thoughts.

If you realize that you have many old negative beliefs, it may be helpful to do some work around releasing them with subconscious belief release techniques including EMDR, hypnotherapy, EFT, Psy-K, or mindful meditation. For further reading and information on this topic, Bruce H. Lipton's *The Biology of Belief: Unleashing the Power of Consciousness, Matter and Miracles*, is a good reference.

The first goal is to apply this directly to yourself because if you change your negative thought and questioning process to be more positive, you will automatically be a better parent for your child. You will break a very old pattern and cycle. You will also see positive benefits in your life overall. The second goal is to begin to ask yourself direct questions whenever you are with your child including:

- What did my child just do right?
- Why do I love my child?
- What is good here?
- In this moment, what can I praise my child for?
- How can I show my child I love them?
- What is the positive of this situation?

As I write these, I remember once again that these questions are so important to ask yourself as well. As adults, we hardly ever acknowledge ourselves and tell ourselves what we are doing right. The only way to create this behavior in yourself is practice, practice, practice.

Remember, there is a HUGE payoff in this way of thinking and interacting with your child—their self-esteem will increase. Your child will believe in themselves and feel empowered. This will impact them their entire life. I promise, it will impact your life as well. After practicing this strategy for the past year, I am now seeing the glass as half full much more often.

1. Create a new practice of asking yourself: "What is my child doing right?", or "What is good about them right now?"
2. Build momentum for this change by putting these questions on your refrigerator, mirror, car or anywhere else you will see them on a regular basis.
3. Ask the same question of yourself – this will create a new pattern in your life.
4. Give yourself positive reinforcement every time you are positive with yourself or your child. I physically pat myself on the back and tell myself I have done well when I have done something I am proud of. It is important for your body to feel this, just as you would reach out to hug your child when you are proud of them and want to connect to them.

5. If you feel frustrated with your child, take a deep breath and count to five. It gives you time to center yourself and to make a better choice of what you want to say to your child.

Allow Your Child To Overhear You

One strategy for positive feedback is to allow your child to "overhear" you saying something positive about them to others. This could occur on a phone conversation or in a conversation with a friend. Here's how it works: while you are talking to another person about how great your child is or what your child has done that makes you proud, make sure your child is close enough to hear what you are saying about them. This can be a very successful and indirect way of building your child's self esteem, especially if they have difficulty hearing positives from you directly.

Write Your Child Notes

Another way to show your child you love them and to give them positive feedback is through notes. Write your child a note and put it in their lunch bag. Send your child a card if you live away from the child telling them how much you love them and what you are proud of them for. You can leave your child notes at home or in their school books. Dry-erase markers for whiteboards work well for writing on mirrors and wash off easy. Any way you can find to tell your child you love them makes your child feel special.

The Day You Were Born

Each year on your child's birthday, wake them up in the morning and tell them a positive story about the day they were born. If both parents were there that day, you will want to include this as it will be so important to your child. You don't have to say a lot but you want to include them somehow. Tell them how you felt. Tell them anything you think is important that they would like to hear. I will never forget my mom telling me that she had not seen my dad cry until the day I was born. These are special memories for your child. Children love to hear positive stories about themselves.

Tell Your Child You Love Them

1. Get on your child's level.
2. Tell them you have something important to tell them.
3. Think about the deep love that you have for your child, really feel these feelings.
4. Look your child in the eyes and tell them how much you love them and why.
5. Give them a hug.

Effective-Parenting Strategy #4: Quality Time With Your Child

It is crucial that when you are with your child, you focus on them. There are a number of ways you can do this.

1. Ask open-ended questions about their life. Ask your child, "What did you do that was fun?" instead of, "Did you have a good time?" The first question is open-ended and asks your child for more information. The second is closed ended—it seeks only a yes or no answer. This is highly effective with teenagers who really don't want to be told things but will respond if you ask their opinion.
2. Focus on the positive when you are with your child.
3. Practice just listening to them.
4. Manage your anger when you are with your child and have patience with them. Always remember they are a child.
5. Teach your child when you are with them. As I walk kids to my office, I say now we will turn to the left and show them with my hand, to the right and show them with my right hand. All moments can be teaching moments if you look for them.
6. Refrain from using your cell phone as much as possible when spending quality time with your child.
7. Limit visitors if you only have limited time with your child.
8. Spend special time with your child one-on-one.
9. Remember to slow down and enjoy your child. Don't over schedule your life. If you have too many things scheduled, you don't enjoy any of them or your child fully.
10. Take time and breathe together. Do the 4-7-8 breathing

technique—count to four as you breathe in, hold your breath for a count of seven, then breathe out as you count to eight—try this exercise together each day. Have your child take a few deep, relaxing breaths before going to sleep.

11. Have a bedtime ritual where you ask your child these questions: 1.) What went well today? 2.) What could have been better? You can also ask them what they are proud of themselves for today.

Effective-Parenting Strategy #5: Conduct Family Meetings To Facilitate Communication

An event that can be very helpful to facilitate building communication and respect in your family is a family meeting. Family meetings give everyone a chance to be heard and to communicate what they need from the family. The following are guidelines for a family meeting:

1. **Time:** Set a specific day and time, no longer than 30 minutes for the meeting and 30 minutes for a fun activity.
2. **Leader Rotates:** The leader should rotate each meeting, the agenda can be listed on a sheet of paper or whiteboard that they can follow each time.
3. **Appreciation/Gratitude:** The meeting should start with appreciations/gratitude. Each person tells what they appreciate about their family or what they appreciated about someone in the family this past week. They can also say what they are grateful for in their family.
   Example: I am grateful that we have been fighting less or I am grateful that dad took us fishing this week.
4. **Problems/Concerns:** The next aspect of the meeting is to discuss concerns/problems. Every member should have a chance to say if they have any concerns or problems for the week. This could also be an opportunity for children to let you know if you are not holding up to your promises of good co-parenting.
   Example: A problem could be that toys are not being

picked up, the hamster keeps escaping or that someone feels left out. Each problem should be documented on a minutes sheet or whiteboard so it can be followed up on in the next meeting.

5. **Action Items**: Go over action items from the previous week that family member agreed to do and what the outcome was (i.e., Joe was to work with Dad to figure out why the hamster was escaping. He says that he was able to figure this out with dad).

6. **Brainstorming:** All the family members should brainstorm solutions to the problem each person brings up to facilitate problem-solving. Come up with as many solutions as possible. The best solution should be agreed upon.

7. **Chores/Contributions/Rules:** Each family member should report on how they are doing with completing their chores and following the rules. If they need any help, they should ask for it here.

8. **Fun:** End the meeting with some type of fun activity the last 30 minutes. You could play a game, make dinner together, go for a walk, go for a bike ride, etc.

 When will you schedule your first Family Meeting?

_____

(Set a date and time)

Effective-Parenting Strategy #6: Have FUN!

It is beyond important that your children have fun in their lives. Sometimes during divorce the fun factor decreases. It is also important for you as an adult to have fun and allow yourself to do things you love. This regenerates your spirit and thus increases your energy for being a healthy parent to your children. It is also crucial that your children have fun. They need to play and have fun to continue their healthy development. It is also important that you have fun together, as a family. Laughing together builds a beautiful bond in your family. Find activities where your family can have fun together.

1. Create a fun-ometer and let your child rate on a scale of

1-10 how you as a family are doing as far as having fun! (see sample in the Appendix). Have your children rate this in your family meeting.

2. Have a CD in the car that has fun and age-appropriate songs on it that you and your child can sing-a-long to and laugh together.
3. Have a joke night where everyone tells jokes to each other.
4. Smile at your children often and remind them to smile. Smiling actually sends a signal to the brain that things are good.
5. Ask your child what they would like to do for fun.

 What is one fun thing I can do with my child this week?

_____

Effective-Parenting Strategy #7: Commit To The Parent's Promise And The Child Of Divorce Promise

The parent's promise is a document created by children of divorce for parents of children of divorce. It outlines the behaviors that will be healthy for your child. Both parents should commit to the other parent that they will uphold these promises. Some parents have used it in their divorce decree and parenting plan. See the Appendix for a copy.

The child of divorce promise was created to assist kids in knowing their role in this process. It was also created so kids can have a voice if they feel put in the middle. For a copy of the Child's Promise see the Appendix. You can go over this promise at your family meetings. This will allow you to check in with your family to ensure they are upholding their promises. It will also allow your children to let you know how they are feeling.

Effective-Parenting Strategy #8: Apologize To Your Child

The bottom line is that you are a parent, and you are trying to be the best possible parent for your child, and you are not perfect. You may make mistakes. An apology that acknowledges these mistakes can build love, trust, and respect. It gives you a blank slate to begin again. Sometimes you may say or do something that later you know was not in the best interest of your child. If this happens, let your child know. You can tell your child something like this:

1. "I know that what I did was not OK. I feel bad and I want you to know that I am sorry." Make a new promise to them if you know you can keep it.

2. You may say something like "I promise that next time when I get that mad, I will take my own time out or I will walk away until things calm down." Just promising not to do it again sets you up to fail if you don't think of ways to change your behavior in the future.

If you have acted negatively towards your child's other parent or argued with the other parent, you can apologize to your child for this. You can also ask them, if they are old enough, to tell you if they feel you are speaking negatively about their other parent or if they feel put in the middle (this can be discussed at the family meeting as well). You can commit to them that you will listen to them and stop. Tell them you are working on this and are committed to not saying anything bad about their other parent, because you know they love their mom/dad. You can also admit it is not nice to say bad things about other people.

Exercise 35. *Apology Exercise*

1. Make a promise right now to yourself that you will apologize to your child if you do something that is not in their best interest.

2. Something happens and you realize it was not in your child's best interest.

3. Think of what you could do to ensure this behavior does not happen again in the future or what would make this behavior less likely to happen. This may include walking away, taking your own self-time, using your own reminders, asking someone else to support you, taking a class, etc.

4. Tell your child you are sorry and that you commit to do better in this area. Make sure that whatever you choose to promise, it is something you can follow through on.

5. As mentioned earlier, if there is something from the past that you want your child's forgiveness for, this exercise also works great. This can even relate to your behavior around the divorce, including talking negatively about your child's other parent.

Method of Apology

Incident:
Dad Yells At Kid

Dad Processes
Incident

Dad
Apologizes

Effective-Parenting Strategy #9: Create Clear Consequences And Take The Emotion Out Of It!

Having pre-set consequences set up with your child can make your life so much easier. Go through all the areas of frustration that are currently causing you stress with your child and use the following methods to set rules, consequences and rewards for behavior.

1. List all of the areas that you want to address with your child. The example we will use is: Clothes are to always be picked up and in the closet or drawers in child's bedroom (be specific here or there will be room for confusion).

2. Decide on consequences if the areas of concern occur. Consequences need to be immediate and important to your child. A consequence for clothes on the floor could be: Limiting screen time by an hour each day clothes are

on the floor. The hour includes them getting the chore done and does not begin until the chore is completed (depending on how long it takes to complete the chore). Screen time is computers, iPods, cell phones, TV, etc.

3. Decide on the reward if your child exhibits the desired behavior for a period of time. An example could be: if clothes are picked up for an entire week, you will allow them to pick a movie of their choice.

4. Have a conversation with your child to set the rules, consequences and rewards.

5. If your child does not do something that you have asked, there will not be a need for anger or frustration. You can simply remind them that there are consequences you have already decided on. You can give them one warning and depending on age you can also count to give them an opportunity to choose another behavior, then you implement the consequence. The worst thing you can do here is not follow through. You must give the consequence every time something is not followed.

6. Be consistent with your promises and follow through. If you don't follow through, you teach your children not to listen to you.

7. You will need to make the choice to not become angry. This may be something you will need to practice. Anger is counter-productive for ourselves and children. Just so you know, you actually choose to be angry. No one else makes us mad, we choose to be angry. If you have trouble in this area, an anger management class may be something to consider.

Effective-Parenting Strategy #10: Teach Your Child To Self Soothe

Children who learn self-soothing methods have better coping skills to assist them as they grow. Self soothing means that children learn ways to help themselves feel better and calm down on their own. This is a lifelong skill that is important to teach your child because your child will not always be able to come to you to be soothed. For young kids this can be a teddy bear that they hug, a fuzzy blanket they lay on, deep breathing or a favorite song they listen to. For older kids this can be a pet that they play with, music they listen to, taking a walk, riding their bike, being outdoors or a cup of hot tea. Children do not need to always be rescued by you, this does not teach them how to help themselves when they are away from you. They need you to help teach them how to deal with certain issues and to self-soothe when they need it.

Effective-Parenting Strategy #11: Recognize and Acknowledge That Children Are Not Bad, They Sometimes Make Bad Choices

No matter what your child does, you still love them. You still love them, you just don't like their choice or behavior. Think about this, make sure it makes sense to you. Make sure your child understands this. Even after you have had to impose a consequence for your child's behavior, you can still end your time with them by saying, "I sometimes may not like the choices you make and I will always love you." You can also say, "I love you and I don't like your behavior." You can also give them a hug.

You are not negating your consequences, you are just keeping your child's self esteem in tact. You are increasing their ability to trust and love in life. Because the truth is that we all make bad choices at times in our lives. You want your child to know that even if they make a bad choice, no matter what, you still love them. And you want them to learn that bad choices yield consequences.

Effective-Parenting Strategy #12: Tell Other Adults Who Are Important in Your Child's Life About the Changes in Your Child's Life

It is extremely important that once you know this transition is occurring in your family that you reach out to other adults who are part of your child's life. Tell coaches, teachers, dance instructors or anyone else in their life who is important. Your child's adjustment-related behaviors may be exhibited in the presence of these adults. Give these important people a heads up about your child's current situation and anything that could cause stress for your child.

Keep in contact with your child's school and pay attention to your child's school performance during and after the divorce. Robert Emory at the University of Virginia found that children of divorced families do not do as well academically as two-parent families in the areas of grades, test scores, school behaviors and school completion.[53]

Sometimes teachers and other adults may see behaviors that you miss or that your child is hiding from you. Adults are understanding of your child during this time. I recently had a teenage client whose parents were arguing so much he could not concentrate to study, so he failed his first eight quizzes in his class. He decided to tell his teacher what was happening and the teacher agreed to allow him to retake all the quizzes. Other people want to help your kids, make sure you make the opportunity available to them and to your child.

Effective-Parenting Strategy #13: Be Available When Your Child Is Ready To Talk To You

A parent I worked with shared, "Inevitably my son never wanted to talk to me until the nights he came home at midnight and I had to get up for work early in the morning." This parent said that every time his son did this, he would wake up and listen. He felt this was very important because if he didn't listen to his son when he was ready to talk, the opportunity may have been lost.

Your children need to know you are there for them when they need you. Of course if this becomes a habit, you may want to discuss it with your child but if it is random, please take the time to listen, especially if it is early in the divorce process. Children need to know you are there for them and will support them when they need it.

Effective-Parenting Strategy #14: Allow And Encourage Your Child To Express Their Feelings

Amazingly, if we just acknowledge how children are feeling, it will help them calm down when they are upset. If your child is not able to verbally express their feelings with words, they may feel even more alienated and misunderstood.[54] This works best for younger children but can work with all ages. An example would be, "Wow, it looks like you are really angry." This is an opening for them to validate this feeling you have observed or tell you that you are wrong, which sometimes happens. Either way, your child feels heard by you.

When we express our feelings, we get them out of our bodies so we can stop reacting to them. It may be hard for you to see your child cry but if they feel like crying, this is good for them. I think one of the biggest mistakes of our society has been to say, "Don't cry." Trauma therapists know that it is so important to cry to release the stress from our body, especially right after a traumatic event. It is OK to have our feelings, that way we don't stuff them in. If we stuff our feelings in, we will need to go back and deal with them later. Many psychologists acknowledge that under anger you usually will find hidden sadness. Sadness pushed down and not expressed can turn to anger. It is crucial for us to acknowledge and express our feelings and to encourage the same for our children.

A feelings chart can be a great resource to use to assist children in identifying their feelings. This could be posted on your refrigerator or anywhere in your home and you could ask your child each morning/evening how they are feeling. Being able to express feelings is important for children and adults. It allows us to connect with ourselves so that we can accurately and effectively express ourselves. Here's a small example. You can also order larger versions at www.healthychildrenofdivorce.com

Feelings Chart (example):

| Happy | Good | OK | Sad | Frustrated | Angry |

Which Bear Do You Feel Like?

Another good method to express feelings is through the use of "I Messages." Using *I Messages* is a tried and tested means of expressing your feelings without putting others on the defensive. This communication technique opens up communication versus shutting it down. It can be used with your children or your children's other parent.

Exercise 36: *I Messages*

I feel _____

When You _____

I would like you to or Please (what you would like from them):

_____

_____

Another *I Message* that you may want to encourage your child to use are *I Need* statements. You could create cards that your child can give to you that have the following needs on them. When your child needs something, the cards may help them to say it.

I need a hug.
I need you to stop fighting.
I need you to do something fun with me.
I need time to myself.
I need you to be nicer to my mom/dad.
I need you to tell me you love me.
I need you to not be angry.
I need you to not say bad things about my other parent.

Your job will be to listen to them and have a discussion with them about their needs and feelings. You can play a game with your child and when they give you a card and are truthful, they will be rewarded somehow.

Effective-Parenting Strategy #15: Establishing Chores And Responsibilities

All children need to know that they are an important member of your family and that they have responsibilities as a child. One way to ensure this happens is to assign them responsibilities and chores that they are responsible for. I define responsibilities as the things that your child needs to do to be responsible and live in your home, such as picking up their clothes, making their bed, helping with dinner, putting away clothes, etc. Chores are defined as things that assist you and make your life easier such as dusting, taking out trash, feeding cat and dog, etc. As a family, you will decide what are responsibilities and what are chores in your family.

All children should have the opportunity to contribute and feel responsible for the success of your family. Chores and being rewarded/praised for their completion can build your child's self esteem. Having chores also teaches them to be responsible, which is a life skill they will use forever. It is important to start them early on responsibilities and chores because if you don't, it may be a battle when they are older. Please see the Appendix for age-appropriate chores and responsibilities. Having chores and responsibilities actually empowers your child as they grow. It is not necessary for you to do things your child can do, this is not healthy. Of course, you will want to provide them positive reinforcement for doing these things. Be clear that tasks that they should do for themselves, such as picking up their room and making their bed, should not be in my opinion, rewarded with money or other things. There should be a consequence if these things are not done. If your child does things over and above that help you such as dusting, feeding dog, vacuuming, you can decide if you want to reward them in some way. For these tasks, you can decide if you want to give them a small allowance or other rewards. The only reason I would agree with an allowance is to teach your child budgeting and money-saving skills. Even if they get $1 a week, you can tell them that they can save 50¢ and spend 50¢. You may want to get them an online bank account where they can see their money grow. See on-line resource at www.healthychildrenofdivorce.com.

Effective-Parenting Strategy #16: Empowering Your Child For Future Success

This summary section provides you with ways that you can empower your child. During this time, your child may feel a lack of control, which can be the truth, they don't have a lot of control right now. However, it is important to empower yourself and your child through the use of some of the following techniques.

1. **Respect Your Child:** See them as the unbelievably intelligent beings that they are. Treat them with respect and allow them to do things for themselves. Don't do everything for them. Doing everything for them is not empowering to children and they don't learn to be empowered adults. Ask their opinion when possible on choices.
2. **Tell Them Positive Things:** Tell them how amazing and brilliant they are. Tell them you know they will grow into a person who is successful and happy. Believe this yourself, your child will grow into this if you facilitate it and believe it.
3. **Take Care of You:** As an adult impacting children in any way, do your own work to ensure you are healthy. Create healthy boundaries for yourself. Make sure to take time for you. Take care of yourself physically. There is a direct correlation between your health and the health of your child.
4. **Take Time with Them Each Day:** Take time with your child each day to focus on them. Ask them, "How are you? What is going well? What is not going well?" Ask if they need anything from you, "Is there anything I could do better?"

Do this age appropriately, of course. If you have a baby, just take time with them and think positive thoughts and tell them positive things. They will hear you and feel your emotion.

5. **Give Them Choices:** Give your child choices whenever possible. Allow them to learn that some choices have consequences. Allow your child to make mistakes. This will enable them to learn and make better future choices.

6. **Create a Positive Vision/Intention For Your Child:** A positive vision/intention could be, "My child _____, is healthy, strong, loving, honest, responsible and peace-filled." Live from what you want for your child, not what you fear or do not want for them. If you are always living in fear of what your child may not be, you can create this for your child. Always intend the positive and not fear the negative. This is important for your life as well.

7. **You Can Do It:** Regularly tell your child, "I know you can do it!" Don't do things for them that they can do for themselves. Assume they have made good choices and decisions. Approach your communication with them from that perspective instead of assuming they need you to tell them what to do. Again, use "I" statements versus "You" orders.

> **"Refrain from anger and turn from wrath; do not fret—it leads only to evil."**
> —Psalm 37:8

8. **Positive Feedback:** Give your child positive feedback daily. Limit your negative comments directed to your child. If your child does something that is not right, ask them what happened and why they did it. Don't assume you know or put your stuff (history, guilt, expectations) on them.

9. **Structure and Responsibility:** Create healthy structures for your child. Make sure they are in bed at an age-appropriate time. Make sure your child does chores to teach them responsibility. You are not empowering or loving your child by doing everything for them. They need to know that you believe they are powerful and strong. They also need

to know what is expected of them and what will happen if expectations are not met. Children thrive and feel safe when they live in a structured environment. They are able to focus on their own development as a child when their environment is safe and structured.

10. **I Love You:** Tell your child verbally and physically (with a hug) that you love them each day.

Empowering your child is truly a fine balance between the positives/teaching moments and the structure/responsibility that children must have in their lives. Children are so amazing. First, we must treat them that way and know that they are strong and intelligent. Second, it is important to give them choices whenever possible. Third, we must set rules, have healthy boundaries and ensure we are creating the best structured environment possible for them to develop and grow. If we do these things, we will be providing the best environment possible for our children to become empowered, peace-filled, and loving adults who know they are capable of doing anything they want in this world.

In summary, if you choose to implement one or two of the above strategies your parenting skills will increase. Your child's ability to grow and develop will be positively impacted. Take a moment now and choose 1–2 of these strategies that you know will benefit you and your family. Share these with your family and practice, practice, practice!

 Now, Commit To It:

I will implement the following two strategies that will assist me in being an even better parent for my child:

1. _____

_____

2. _____

_____

⚜ ⚜ ⚜

Questions For Reflection:

What do I know is crucial for me to do for my child?

_____

_____

What didn't I get as a child that I now can do for myself
(positive reinforcement, fun, etc.)

_____

_____

_____

_____

_____

_____

_____

_____

_____

_____

_____

_____

_____

_____

_____

_____

_____

~~10~~

Hope For The Future

My intent for this book has been to give you hope. A wise person once said that there is a difference between individuals who believe they can't change and those who know change is possible. Individuals who know change is possible have something very important—they have hope. In my heart of hearts, I have a deep hope that divorce can be friendly to our children. I have hope that parents will make different choices and decisions for the sake of their children. I have hope that you and your family will heal and grow from this event.

I have hope for and believe in your family. As a child, I did not have that for my family. I was just trying to survive the conflict in my family. My goal is not for your child to survive but to thrive with two healthy parents. I know that if you have picked up this book, you are one of the parents who can create change, someone who has hope for a better future for your children. You believe in yourself and I believe in you. Statistics tell us that if your child has just one stable parent, they have a better chance of succeeding in life. If the journey gets too challenging or you feel as if you are losing hope, please reach out for help. Find someone in your life that is only a phone call away. Know that so many resources including myself are only an email or phone call away. The on-line divorce forum is just a click away at www. healthychildrenofdivorce.com. Accept support from others, it will change your life.

There are a few key points that I want to leave you with. They are the very good news that you can carry with you as you step into your new future.

You Have A Choice

You have a choice in how you move forward in parenting your child. You choose how you react to your child's other parent. Remember, no one else can ever truly make you angry, you make a choice to become angry. This gives you a lot of power. If you choose not to react angrily to something your child's other parent says, in effect, you win. Their goal might be to make you angry and if you make another choice, they have not accomplished their goal and you win. Remember to "take the high road." It will payoff.

You Can Decide To Forgive And Move Forward

Forgiveness does not mean that you forget what someone did. Forgiveness also does not mean that what someone else did was right. It means that you no longer choose to hold anger and resentment towards them. Always remember that any anger you hold and forgiveness you withhold, only hurts you.

Because this anger hurts you, it also hurts your child. The person you are angry at could quite possibly care less. There is huge freedom for you in forgiveness. I was recently in India and participated with some friends in Yom Kippur, which is the Jewish Holiday of forgiveness. The Jewish faith has one day a year to honor and celebrate forgiveness. Make today a day of forgiveness, whether it is choosing to forgive someone else or asking someone else to forgive you. You may be surprised at how many people you have to forgive once you begin looking at this. Just be open to forgiveness and you will probably find more people than you can think of at this moment. I also believe that you must forgive yourself. The first person you may want to focus on is you. What do you need to forgive yourself for? Ideas may be: marrying the wrong man; choosing the wrong woman; being a less-than-perfect parent; or not fulfilling a commitment made to God. Holding these things without forgiving yourself only does you harm and does not create space for you to live in peace

"Remember to 'take the high road.' It will payoff."

and freedom. My wish for you is that you find this peace and freedom.

Past, Present And Future

I truly believe that all we have is the present moment. If we are thinking about (or dwelling on) the past or worrying about the future, we are not living to our full potential. What this means is that right now, in this present moment, you can decide to make changes in your life and to do it differently. Declare the past complete and choose to leave it there. At this point, nothing can be done and it is only wasting energy to focus on it. Begin to live today using what you have learned from this book. Put one or two things into practice right now. You can make a choice to do it differently, for your child's future. Your child's future is being created right now, in this moment, with the choices you make. Please look at your choices as not about you and your ego, but see them as being about your child and your family you now have with your child. I truly know you have done your best up to this point and now with this knowledge, it is time to make even better choices. Life is too short for anything less.

A Better Way, Taking The Journey Of Love

Do you want your child to feel secure knowing that they received the best love and guidance from their parents? Or do you want them to be fearful that they may never make a good decision, never have a good relationship, never make a good mother or father, never be successful or never truly be able to love themselves or others?

> **"You are your child's first and most influential teacher."**
> —M. Gary Neuman

The decisions you make each moment with your children and how you choose to act will impact these huge life goals in your children's lives. I know, I am a child of divorce and conflict. My wish for your child is to endure less pain than other children I know and whom I counsel today. Know in your heart that you have the ability to make new and good choices every moment. You are strong and powerful. Your children are counting on you as their guidepost in life to make decisions that will provide them with the opportunity to be the happiest and most productive adult possible. I know that sometimes this can feel like a very scary proposition. I have complete faith in you. You are not alone in this journey.

Cast A Pebble In The Pond

Let all of us, in our own unique way, recommit ourselves to the search for the pebbles of change that can be cast into the social pond. Let us create a divorce process that recycles divorce pain into new patterns of personal and familial growth which, in turn, will also strengthen our entire society. Let us protect our children from the unnecessary hazards of the divorce experience so that they, like their parents, can be strengthened by divorce rather than defeated by it. And let us never forget that if the lights go out in our children's eyes, be they children of divorce or any other children, we will all live in darkness.

—Meyer Elkin, Editor AFCC

I wrote this book for your children. I have witnessed and understand their pain first-hand, as a child who lived through it, and through my work. My encouragement to you is to heal yourself and believe in yourself. Taking care of you is the first step to really taking care of your children. I know you are already a good parent and have what it takes to be the best co-parent you can be. I thank you from the bottom of my heart for the difference you will make in the world for your child's sake and for all the lives your child will touch. Being a parent is the most important job in the world. I thank you for your commitment to do one of the most important jobs in the best possible way you can. Your child thanks you and the world thanks you. It is how we treat our children that will determine the fate of the world. What do you want our world to look like in 20 years? 50 years? 100 years? I encourage you to take a stand for yourself and your child right now, begin your healing and begin the journey of life. I ask you to do the last exercise to step into your new life. You deserve it. You are the hope. You can choose to make choices that create hope for your children and for our world.

Final Exercise

For this exercise, you should be standing. Envision in front of you an imaginary line. This is a deciding line. Everything on your side of the line is the past, it is everything you have gone through up until now. Now think of everything you want to step into, your new life, the new way of being a co-parent, the life you want for your child. All of this is the future and it is on the other side of that line. Envision all that you want. Think about how you will feel when you have this. Close your eyes and focus on that feeling now. When you are ready, take a huge step and step across that line into your future. You are stepping into your future and the future of your child. Don't look back, don't worry how you will create it, just do it. Make the choice every step of the way to step into your future of love, peace and freedom. This is my first and last wish for you.

> **"I have learned over the years that when one's mind is made up, this diminishes fear; knowing what must be done does away with fear."**
> —Rosa Parks,
> American Civil Rights leader

Question For Reflection:

What impact do I want to have in this world?

_____

_____

_____

_____

_____

_____

_____

_____

_____

_____

_____

_____

_____

_____

_____

_____

_____

_____

_____

_____

_____

_____

_____

APPENDIX

A. Letter To My Co-Parent

B. Age-Appropriate Responsibilities and Chores

C. Parent's Promise

D. Child's Promise

E. Developmental Ages and Stages

F. Fun-ometer

G. Feelings Chart (print and post)

H. Anger Scale

I. Parenting Plan (Sample)

J. Taking Responsibility

K. Co-Parent Invitation To Participate
    (Letter From Shannon R. Rios)

For downloadable copies of these documents, visit
www.healthychildrenofdivorce.com

A. LETTER TO MY CO-PARENT

To My Co-Parent:

Thank you for taking the time to read this letter. I am sending this letter to you because I just read *The 7 Fatal Mistakes Divorced and Separated Parents Make: Strategies for Raising Healthy Children of Divorce* by Shannon Rios, MS LMFT. Shannon was a child of a high-conflict marriage and divorce. She speaks from her heart and with the knowledge she has gained working with families of divorce and conflict.

Reading this book, I realize that I want to do some things different so our child is not negatively impacted by our separation/divorce. I realize I have said and done some things that have not been in our child's best interest. I have made a commitment to do things differently for the best interest of our child _____. Our child deserves this.

I love our child so much and I know you do, too. Can we please arrange a time where we can talk calmly, where our entire focus is our child and what we can better do as co-parents to help them adjust to this transition.

Together, we created this amazing child. My goal is to put our differences aside so we can focus on what is best for him/her. I also want to apologize to you for _____
_____   _____
_____

I have learned that holding on to anger at another person and not forgiving them only hurts me and our child. I choose to let go of any anger that has been a part of our relationship. My goal is to live a peaceful and happy life. I want us both to do that separate because that will be the healthiest thing for our child. They will get to have the best life possible if we do this.

You are my child's parent, I respect that and I want us both to do all that we can to ensure our child has the best possible future. _____deserves that from us because we are her/his parents.

I thank you for considering this, I realize it may be challenging. I am confident that we can do this to support the amazing child we created together. Even small changes could make a huge difference for our child. I thank you for being our child's parent. Just because of our choices, I do not want our child to suffer. I thank you for (a positive quality about your other parent) _____

I have also included a copy of The Parent's Promise and I agree to uphold all of these promises as we raise our child as Co-parents.

In our child's best interest,

_____(your signature)

B. AGE-APPROPRIATE CHORES FOR CHILDREN

Responsibilities are items your child should be responsible for as a team member of your family.

Chores are extra items that help you out as a parent. Each family may view these differently.

Allowance is only recommended for chores.

Age (Years)	Chores and Responsibilities
2-3	• Pick up toys and books (responsibility) • Throw away trash in wastebasket (responsibility) • Put laundry in correct place (responsibility) • Help feed family pet (chore)
3-4	• Help to set table (responsibility/chore) • Help care for (well-behaved) family pet (chore) • Put toys away (responsibility)
4-5	• Make bed with help (responsibility) • Set table (responsibility) • Bring in mail (chore) • Get dressed (responsibility) • Empty wastebasket (responsibility) • Brush hair, brush teeth, dress (responsibility)
5-6	• Make bed (less than perfect) (responsibility) • Make sure bedroom is picked up (responsibility) • Care more for family pet (chore) • Answer telephone (responsibility) • Care of plants, water with assistance (chore) • Put clean clothes in drawers/closets (responsibility)

6-8	• Use alarm clock to wake up (responsibility) • Help pack cold lunch (responsibility) • Wash self/keep self clean (responsibility) • Rinse dirty dishes and load into dishwasher (chore) • Take phone messages (responsibility) • Clean bedroom (responsibility) • Help with kitchen clean up (responsibility) • Wipe off sink in bathroom after use (responsibility)
8-12	• Bring out garbage for pick-up (chore) • Wash and dry dishes (chore) • Vacuum (chore) • Clean kitchen counters and sink (chore) • Care for pet (responsibility/chore) • Run dishwasher (responsibility/chore) • Clean Bathroom (responsibility/chore)
12+	• Baby sitting siblings for short periods of time (chore) • Change bed sheets (responsibility) • Shovel snow (chore) • Wash and dry clothes (responsibility) • Assist with preparation of simple meals (responsibility)

C. THE PARENT'S PROMISE

Written by Children of Divorce for Children of Divorce
For The Greatest Good Of My Child

I Hereby Agree That:

1. I will not speak negatively about my child's other parent to my child.
2. I will not say to my child "that (insert negative behavior or characteristic) is just like your father/mother".
3. I agree to not put my child in the middle of issues I have with the other parent (especially child support).
4. I agree to not use my child as a pawn to get back at their other parent.
5. I agree that if my child's other parent has a new relationship; I will not speak negatively of this other person to my child.
6. I will not expect my child to take care of me when I am upset.
7. I will periodically ask my child how he or she is doing.
8. I will do my best to fully support my child during this process.
9. I will allow my child to be a child during this time.
10. I will seek outside professional counseling if I need to speak with someone about this situation or if I am having difficulty maintaining this agreement.
11. I agree that if I do not uphold the above promises that I personally am not acting in the best interest of my child's physical and emotional health.
12. I will speak with my child's coach/counselor once a month to gain further insight.

By agreeing to the Parent's Promise, I am accepting responsibility as a parent to provide the best environment possible during this transition for my child. In upholding these promises, I am also acknowledging to my child that they have no fault in this decision that was made by their parents. I am fully committed to the best interest of my child's emotional and physical health during this time and to their future growth and development.

Honestly and with much love, I commit to this for my child.

_____

Signature

D. THE CHILD'S PROMISE

Written by Children of Divorce for Children of Divorce

So That I Can Be The Amazing Child That I Am:

1. I promise to have fun and play!
2. I promise to be a kid and not worry about my parents, that is not my job.
3. I promise to tell my mom, dad or counselor if I am scared, angry, sad or feeling bad.
4. I promise to remember the divorce is not my fault.
5. I promise to tell my parents if I feel put in the middle.
6. I promise to remember I am special each day.
7. I promise to smile each day.
8. I promise to remember it is OK to love both of my parents.
9. I promise to tell my parents how I am feeling.
10. I promise to tell my parents what I need from them!

Signature

E. DEVELOPMENTAL AGES AND STAGES

Age (Years)	Characteristics of this Age and Stage	Challenges— Reaction to Stress and Change	What Child Needs from Parent of Divorce
0-3	- Building foundation of trust - Building relationships - Need predictability, consistency and routine - At the end of this stage, child is struggling to assert their independence - Child later in this stage tests limits to see what adult will do remember to "take the high road," by providing limits and safety; it will payoff - Child is very egocentric at this age	- Child may express frustration through behaviors and emotions - Child may regress and have developmental delays - Symptoms include problems with feeding, sleeping and self-soothing - Child may become irritable, depressed or withdrawn - May feel insecure	- Provide security, love, support, flexibility and consistency - Parents that are calm and soothing - If possible (and child has not been in daycare before), wait to put child in daycare until things are calm in the family - If there has been only one primary caregiver, depending on child, age for overnights will vary - Child may have 2 or 3 primary caregivers - Parents that don't fight when exchanging custody, this also stresses babies because caregivers are stressed

| 3-5 | - Development of thinking skills and friendships
- In wonder of everything
- Preparing for school
- Child closely watches grown-ups to see adults' actions and reactions
- Child will usually have a lot of questions | - May regress in areas of toileting, sleeping and eating
- May be cranky and clingy
- May be sad, afraid and withdrawn
- May worry about parents
- May want to sleep with parent
- May be confused | - Reassurance that parent is OK
- Predictability, routine and structure
- Can usually do overnights but depends on child and relationship with parent
- Neutral exchange site if parents are conflicting
- Spend nurturing time with child, holding, speaking soothing words and rocking
- Parents pick them up on time
- Assurance from parent that they will be there when child returns
- Make sure child knows that they don't have to choose
- Calendar to see the schedule
- Depend on parent for comfort
- Understanding that they did not cause divorce
- Help child to develop their ability to self-soothe
- Help child to learn to be responsible for their own things |

Contact:
Shannon@LifeThreads.net or 303-284-3431

6-12	- Friendships growing - Social skill developing - Learning to express feelings - Self-esteem grows when child is successful in school, play and family - Learning skills in other areas, sports, dance, music and art - Children develop a clear sense of what is right and wrong and parent is there to assist child in supporting the values child is developing - Child wants to feel they are important	- May experience anger/hostility - May feel powerless - Tantrums - Regression - Sleep problems - Problems in school - Withdrawal or aggressive with peers - May become overwhelmed - May be disorganized - May fear abandonment* - May have increased irritability and aggression*	- Structure and routine esp. for school, includes average of 11 hours of sleep per night - Rules in the home - Reassurance that you are OK and what you are doing to take care of yourself - Need reassurance they are not responsible for divorce - Not to be put in middle or involved in parents anger - Neutral exchange site if parents are conflicting - Calendar to see the schedule - Space in the new home to call their own - Ability to continue or develop new social activities - Clarify that their job as a child is to have fun, have friends and go to school - Allow child to have choices to feel more powerful - Attend child's sporting events, performances, school plays, etc. - Make sure child has responsibilities and chores

*Heatherington, et al, 1982

| 13-17 | - Task is to develop independence and separation from family
- Discuss future goals with family
- Driving and dating
- Going through a lot of physical, social and emotional changes
- Begins to form own identity
- Dependence on friends grows
- Becomes less involved with the family | - Oppositional and negative
- May feel loneliness and abandonment
- Over-whelmed
- Risk for academic failure
- Eating and sleeping disorders
- Relationships with opposite sex
- Jealousy of parents new partner
- Pregnancy/ promiscuity
- Mood swings
- Depression
- Delinquency
- Substance abuse
- May detach from family
- Gangs | - Limit amount of conflict
- Find time to spend time one on one with your child
- If extreme conflict in family and teen detaches, teen needs support from others, teachers, family members, therapist
- Rules and routine
- Chores and responsibilities in home
- Discussion about dating and expectations
- Discussion on use of drugs and alcohol
- Parents understanding that as child grows, they will spend less time with the parent, this is normal
- Consistent routines, not too much freedom
- Boundaries for safety
- Parental involvement very important
- Discussion of birth control (boys and girls) or family thoughts on intercourse
- Connecting time with parents one on one
- Attend child's sporting events, performances, school plays, etc. |

F. FUN-OMETER

Use the Fun-Ometer to measure the level of fun your family is currently having. Periodically ask your child how your family is doing at bringing fun into your lives.

G. FEELINGS CHART

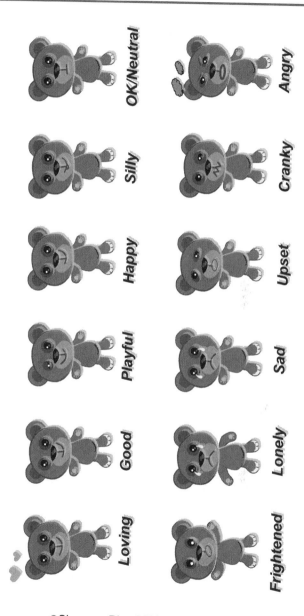

H. ANGER SCALE

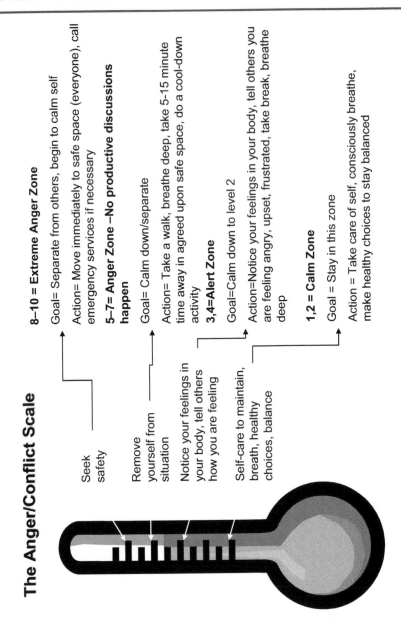

The Anger/Conflict Scale

8–10 = Extreme Anger Zone

Goal= Separate from others, begin to calm self

Action= Move immediately to safe space (everyone), call emergency services if necessary

5–7= Anger Zone –No productive discussions happen

Goal= Calm down/separate

Action= Take a walk, breathe deep, take 5-15 minute time away in agreed upon safe space, do a cool-down activity

3,4=Alert Zone

Goal=Calm down to level 2

Action=Notice your feelings in your body, tell others you are feeling angry, upset, frustrated, take break, breathe deep

1,2 = Calm Zone

Goal = Stay in this zone

Action = Take care of self, consciously breathe, make healthy choices to stay balanced

Seek safety

Remove yourself from situation

Notice your feelings in your body, tell others how you are feeling

Self-care to maintain, breath, healthy choices, balance

I. SAMPLE PARENTING PLAN

On this date _____/_____/_____, We, _____
and _____, the mother and father of
_____ agree to the following plan in order to ensure
_____ 's optimal development. We wish to provide
continuity, stability and predictability for _____ while
ensuring that he/she will have frequent and continuing contact with
each parent.

1. *Joint Decision-making:* We agree to jointly make all decisions
   regarding _____ 's education, health, and general
   welfare. We agree that all day to day decisions will be made
   individually.

2. *Communication:* The parents agree to communicate on a
   regular basis regarding the needs and welfare of their children
   _____ _____ so that he/she/they
   are not messengers and therefore do not feel responsible for any
   misunderstandings that may arise. We agree to communicate in the
   following manner: (i.e., Wednesday at 9am we will have a call to
   discuss issues related to the children/child) _____
   _____ _____
   _____

3. We agree that we will resolve the holidays and scheduling 30-days
   prior to the start of each calendar year.

4. *Medical Emergencies:* Each parent has the ability to obtain
   emergency health care for their children/child without the consent
   of the other parent. Each parent shall notify the other parent as
   soon as possible if an illness or injury requires a physician's care.
   All matters for surgery or major medical or dental work shall be
   discussed and resolved before the work is started, when possible.

5. *If either parent will be absent from the home overnight while _____ is/are in his/her custody, the other parent will be advised and given the opportunity to care for him/her/them before other arrangements are made.*

6. *If the opportunity is taken advantage of, the other parent agrees to an equal exchange at his/her convenience within _____months of the agreement.*

7. *Each parent will provide the other with the addresses and telephone number of the residence where the child will be while with the parent. Reasonable notice will be provided for any anticipated travel and itineraries will be provided. Reasonable notice is considered _____*

8. *Each parent will be allowed reasonable telephone communication with _____. Each parent will respect their child's right to privacy during these conversations.*

The parents will share custody of their children according to the following physical custody plan:

Holidays and Special Days:

Day:	With Parent:
Martin Luther King Jr. Day	
President's Day	
Spring Vacation	
Mother's Day Weekend	
Memorial Day	
Father's Day Weekend	
July 4th	
Labor Day	
Thanksgiving Vacation	
Christmas Vacation	
Other School Days Off	
Other: • • •	

Three-Day Weekends:

It is our intent that each year's three-day weekends be spent equally in each home. We will meet in _____ to review the year's balance and adjust in the final three months if any imbalance exists.

Summer School Vacation:

Same basic schedule except for family vacation trips on an exchange basis and agreed upon by (list preferred vacation dates):

Mother's preference _____

Father's preference _____

Basic Schedule:

Name of Child:	Days/Schedule

School Events and Activities:

Each parent shall be responsible for keeping himself/ herself advised of all school, athletic or social events in which _____ participates. Each parent will be responsible for arranging for joint meetings with their child's/ children's individual teachers, whether requested by the parent or the teacher. Major school activities and all matters with school/parent communications should be shared.

1. Except as otherwise agreed between the parents, each parent shall pick up the child/children at the beginning of each of his or her physical custody periods.

2. In the event that a decision cannot be made jointly by us, we propose to submit the differences to a mediator.

3. Each parent will at all times make every effort to maintain free access and contact between _____ and his/ her/their other parent and agree to promote a feeling of goodwill between his/her/their other parent. Neither parent will do

anything to diminish the relationship that the child has with their other parent that would impair the child's love and respect for each of them.

Continuity Agreement Between Households:

Bedtime, school nights	
Bedtime, non-school nights	
Wake-up Time School Mornings	
Limitations on TV and Video Viewing	
Personal Hygiene (tooth-brushing, bathing, shampoos)	
Homework time	
School preparation	
Scheduling extra-curricular activities	

J. TAKING RESPONSIBILITY

THE CHOICE TO LIVE A POWERFUL LIFE

1. I (somehow) chose this other person as my child's other parent.
2. I choose to forgive the other parent for the past.
3. I choose to forgive myself.
4. I choose to be a parent
5. I choose to let go of anger and move forward with my life.
6. I choose to be the best parent possible for my child.
7. I choose to allow my child to freely love both of his/her parents and relatives.
8. I choose to find something positive in my child's other parent.
9. If I need assistance with any of the above, I choose to ask for and accept help.
10. I choose my child. I choose to provide my child with the best foundation for their most amazing life.
11. I choose a good relationship with my child, forever.
12. I choose to take this journey one day at a time and be kind to myself each day.

Signed in great love for me and my child.

K. CO-PARENT INVITATION TO PARTICIPATE
(Letter From Shannon R. Rios)

Dear Co-Parent of Divorce/Separation:
You are receiving this letter because your co-parent recently read my book, The 7 Fatal Mistakes Divorcing Parents Make: Strategies for Raising Healthy Children of Divorce. In the book, I asked them to make a lot of difficult choices and I asked them to act in the best interest of your child. This letter is one of the ways I recommended they do that.

I wrote my book because I am a child of divorce. I went through, watched my sisters go through, and saw countless other families go through the pain of divorce and conflict due to parents' anger at each other. In my heart, I want for every child to have the easiest and healthiest divorce experience possible. Your child deserves that from you. They did nothing to choose this situation. All they have ever done is love both of their parents. And it tears them apart to see you and your former partner angry and fighting with each other.

Your co-parent has realized that they want to make changes in the way the two of you are co-parenting your child together. They want to make these changes because they love your child. They also know that you love your child as well. Undoubtedly, you have both hurt each other. The hurt is never one-sided. It is time now to put the hurt aside and move forward for your child.

You are receiving this letter because your co-parent wants to discuss with you how the two of you can work together for the best interest of your child and their future. What I do know is that parents want the best for their children. All parents make mistakes, my heartfelt advice is for you to realize this and move forward. Leave any anger you are carrying behind because, in the end, it only hurts you and your child. If you can let the anger go, your child will thank you in the end.

Please consider having a discussion about your co-parenting relationship with your child's other parent, if for no other reason than the love you have in your heart for your child. This discussion should be only about your child, and nothing else. The bottom line is that your child will always love you both and the greatest gift you can give them is to be parents who can make decisions in their best interest, not out of anger at the other parent.

I write this letter for your child, for you and your co-parent. May you move forward into a peaceful and happy life. I always remember the quote: "Resentment is like taking your own poison and hoping the other person will die." It is your choice to live a life of forgiveness and peace. I have included my Parent's Promise. If you think you cannot commit to these, I encourage you to talk to a professional who can help you through this process.

If you have any questions, please feel free to contact me or one of my associates. We can also help facilitate this process for you. I can assure you that the investment you make will be worth its weight in gold to your child and their happiness.

In Gratitude for Your Amazing Child,

Shannon R Rios, MS LMFT

BIBLIOGRAPHY

Adams, Marilee G. PhD. *Change Your Questions, Change Your Life: 10 Powerful Tools for Life and Work.* 2d edition. San Francisco: Berrett-Koehler Publishers, 2009.

Anderson, Susan. *The Journey From Abandonment to Healing: Turning the End of a Relationship into a New Life.* New York: Berkley Publishing Group, 2000.

Bays, Brandon. *The Journey: A Practical Guide to Healing Your Life and Setting Yourself Free.* New York: Fireside, 2002.

Benedek, E.P. MD. & C.F. Brown, M.Ed. *How to Help Your Child Overcome Your Divorce. A Support Guide for Families.* New York: Newmarket Press, 1998.

Gardner, R.A., MD. *The Parents Book About Divorce.* New York: Bantam Books, 1991.

Hannibal, Mary Ellen, *Good Parenting Through Your Divorce: How to Recognize, Encourage, and Respond to Your Child's Feelings and Help Them Get Through Your Divorce.* New York: Marlowe & Company, 2002.

Hendrix, H. PhD. *Getting the Love You Want: A Guide for Couples.* New York: Holt and Company, 1998, 2008.

Hetheringon EM, Cox, M, Cox R: Effects of divorce on parents and children. In ME Lamb (ed.) *Non Traditional Families: Parenting And Child Development.* Hillsdale, NJ: Erlbaum, 1982.

Hetherington EM and Kelly, John. *For Better or For Worse: Divorce Reconsidered.* New York: W.W. Norton and Company, 2002.

Hickey, E., MSW & Dalton, E. JD. *Healing Hearts: Helping Children and Adults Recover from Divorce.* Seattle, WA: Gold Leaf Press, 1997.

Jones-Soderman, J. & Quattrocchi, A. *How to Talk to Your Children About Divorce: Understanding What Your Children May Think, Feel and Need.* Family Mediation Publishing Co.: Scottsdale, AZ. 2006.

Kalter, N. PhD. *Growing Up With Divorce: Helping Your Child Avoid Immediate and Later Emotional Problems.* Free Press: New York. 1990.

Kelly, Joan B. *Risk and Resiliency for Children of Separation and Divorce: Current Research and Implications for Practice.* Presentation at Loyola University, Chicago IL, June 2005.

Lansky, Vicki. *Vicki Lansky's Divorce Book for Parents.* Minnetonka, MN: Book Peddlers, 2003.

Lipton, Bruce H. PhD. *The Biology of Belief: Unleashing the Power of Consciousness, Matter and Miracles.* Carlsbad, CA: Hay House, 2008.

Long, N, PhD. & R. Forehand, PhD. *Making Divorce Easier on Your Child: 50 Effective Ways to Help Children Adjust.* Chicago: Contemporary Books, 2002.

Marquardt, E. *Between Two Worlds: The Inner Lives of Children of Divorce.* New York: Three Rivers Press, 2005.

Marston, S. *The Divorced Parent: Success Strategies for Raining Your Children After Separation.* New York: William Morrow and Company, 1994.

Mate, Gabor, M.D. *How Attention Deficit Disorder Originates and What You Can Do About It.* New York: Plume, 1999.

McGraw, Phil. PhD. *Love Smart: Find the One You Want, Fix the One You Got.* New York: Free Press, 2005.

Neuman, M.G. & P. Romanowski. *Helping Your Kids Cope With Divorce the Sandcastles Way.* New York: Random House, 1998.

Oddenino, Michael L. *Putting Kids First: Walking Away From a Marriage Without Walking All Over the Kids.* Family Connections Publishing: USA, 1995.

Ross, J.A, M.A. & J. Corcoran. *Joint Custody with a Jerk: Raising a Child with an Uncooperative Ex.* New York: St. Martin's Press, 1996.

Schneider, M.F. & Zuckerberg, J. PhD. *Difficult Questions Kids Ask: And Are Too Afraid to Ask About Divorce.* New York: Fireside, 1996.

Stahl, P.M. PhD. *Parenting After Divorce: A Guide to Resolving Conflicts and Meeting Your Children's Needs.* Atascadero, CA: Impact Publishers, 2000.

Thich Nat Hanh. *True Love: A Practice for Awakening the Heart.* Boston: Shambala Publications, 1997.

Thomas, S. PhD. *Parents Are Forever: A Step-by-Step Guide to Becoming Successful Coparents After Divorce.* Longmont, CO: Springboard Publications, 2004.

Thomas, S. PhD. *Two Happy Homes: A Working Guide for Parents & Stepparents After Divorce and Remarriage.* Longmont, CO: Springboard Publications, 2005

Wallerstein, J. S. & S. Blakeslee. *What About the Kids? Raising Your Children Before, During and After Divorce.* New York: Hyperion, 2003.

Wallerstein, J.S., J. M. Lewis, & S. Blakeslee. *The Unexpected Legacy of Divorce: A 25-Year Landmark Study.* New York: Hyperion, 2000.

Welwood, John. *Perfect Love: Imperfect Relationships.* Boston: Trumpeter, 2007.

Woodward Thomas, K. *Calling In The One: 7 Weeks to Attract the Love of Your Life.* New York: Three Rivers Press, 2004.

NOTES

1. Wallerstein, J. S. & Blakeslee, S. *What About the Kids? Raising Your Children Before, During and After Divorce.* New York: Hyperion, 2003
2. Hetherington EM and Kelly, J. *For Better or For Worse: Divorce Reconsidered.* New York: W.W. Norton and Company, 2002
3. Ahrons, Constance. "We're Still Family: What Grown Children Have to Say About Their Parent's Divorce." *Colorado Springs Gazette*, June 7, 2004
4. Marston, Stephanie. *The Divorced Parent: Success Strategies for Raising Your Children After Separation.* New York: William Marrow and Company, Inc., 1994
5. Kelly, Joan B. *Risk and Resiliency for Children of Separation and Divorce: Current Research and Implications for Practice*, Chicago: Loyola University, June 2005
6. Ross, J & Corcoran, J, *Joint Custody With a Jerk: Raising a Child With an Uncooperative Ex.* New York, 1996
7. Hickey, E., M.S.W & Dalton, E. J.D. *Healing Hearts: Helping Children and Adults Recover from Divorce.* Seattle, WA: Gold Leaf Press, 1997
8. Kelly, 2005
9. Ibid.
10. Gumby's image is used with permission, courtesy of the Prema Toy Co., Inc. All rights reserved. Prema Toy Co., Inc. © 2009
11. Wallerstein, 2003
12. Long, N, PhD. & R. Forehand, Ph.D. *Making Divorce Easier on Your Child: 50 Effective Ways to Help Children Adjust.* Chicago: Contemporary Books, 2002
13. Hickey & Dalton, 1997
14. Hannibal, Mary Ellen, *Good Parenting Through Your Divorce: How to Recognize, Encourage, and Respond to Your Child's Feelings and Help Them Get Through Your Divorce.* New York: Marlowe & Company, 2002
15. Thomas, S. PhD. *Parents Are Forever: A Step-by-Step Guide to Becoming Successful Coparents After Divorce.* Longmont, CO: Springboard Publications, 2004
16. Lansky, Vicki. *Vicki Lansky's Divorce Book for Parents.* Minnetonka, MN: Book Peddlers, 2003
17. Tufts University, 1988
18. Kelly, 2005
19. Schneider, M.F. & Zuckerberg, J. PhD. *Difficult Questions Kids Ask: And Are Too Afraid to Ask About Divorce.* New York: Fireside, 1996
20. Lansky, 2003
21. Kelly, 2005
22. Marquart, E. *Between Two Worlds: The Inner Lives of Children of Divorce.* New York: Three Rivers Press, 2005
23. Hannibal, 2002
24. Long and Forehand, 2002

25. Wallerstein, et al., *The Unexpected Legacy of Divorce: A 25-Year Landmark Study.* New York: Hyperion, 2000

26. Schneider & Zuckerberg, 2001

27. Richard Gardner, MD. *The Parents Book About Divorce.* New York: Bantam Books, 1991

28. Wallerstein, 2003

29. U.S. Department of Health and Human Services Substance Abuse and Mental Health Services Administration Center for Mental Health Services. www.mentalhealth.samhsa.gov. SAMHSA's National Mental Health Information Center.

30. Thomas, 2001

31. Wallerstein, 2007

32. Garner, 1991

33. Stahl, P.M., 2000

34. Kalter, 1990

35. Hannibal, 2002

36. Gardner, 1991

37. Hannibal, 2002

38. Hannibal, 2002

39. Gardner, 1991

40. Many psychologists agree it takes 21 days to change a behavior into a habit or to eliminate the behavior entirely. This article from Florida International Univ. discusses changing/eliminating a bad habit in 21 days—http://www.fiu.edu/~oea/InsightsFall2004/online_library/articles/daily%20activities%20to%20help%20change%20habits.htm

41. Wallerstein, 2003

42. Hannibal, 2002

43. Wallerstein, 2007

44. Jones-Soderman and Quattrocchi, 1996

45. Oddenino, M.L. *Putting Kids First: Walking Away From a Marriage Without Walking All Over the Kids.* Family Connections Publishing: USA, 1995

46. McGraw, Phil PhD, *Love Smart*, New York: Free Press, 2005, p. 74

47. Mental Health America 2000 N. Beauregard Street, 6th Floor Alexandria, VA 22311 http://www.mentalhealthamerica.net/go/codependency.

48. Ibid.

49. Foster Cline, "Developing Mile Hi Character in Our Children," presentation at Mile Hi Church, January 23, 2009

50. Jones-Soderman and Quattrocchi, 2006

51. Hickey, 1997

52. Marston, 1994

53. Long and Forehand, 2002

54. Neuman, 1988

Know someone who needs to read
The 7 Fatal Mistakes Divorced & Separated Parents Make
Order them a copy!

Payment can be with credit card via phone or you can send check to address below.

Order By:

TELEPHONE: Call 1-303-720-6534

WEB: www.healthychildrenofdivorce.com

MAIL: Complete form below and send
with check or money order for $23.90
(includes $3.95 shipping and handling) to:
LifeThreads Publishing
PO Box 2471, Evergreen, CO 80437

Please send more FREE LifeThreads information on:
□ Speaking/Seminars
□ Coaching/Consulting

Name: _____

Address: _____

_____

_____

City/State/Zip: _____

Organization: _____

Phone#: _____

Email: _____

For International or Overnight Orders (additional shipping charges may apply): Please call 1-303-720-6534

www.healthychildrenofdivorce.com